Words in Sheep's Clothing

OTHER BOOKS BY MARIO PEI

All About Language
The America We Lost
The Book of Place Names (with E. Lambert)
The Families of Words
First-Year French (with E. Méras)
Getting Along in French (with J. Fisher)
Getting Along in German (with R. Politzer)
Getting Along in Italian
Getting Along in Russian (with F. Nikanov)
Getting Along in Spanish (with E. Vaquero)
Glossary of Linguistic Terminology
How to Learn Languages and What Languages to Learn
Invitation to Linguistics
The Italian Language
The Language of the Eighth-Century Texts in Northern France
Language for Everybody
Language Today (with others)
The Many Hues of English
One Language for the World
Our Names (with E. Lambert)
Our National Heritage
The Story of the English Language
The Story of Language
Swords of Anjou
Talking Your Way Around the World
Voices of Man
What's in a Word?
The World's Chief Languages

MARIO PEI

Words in Sheep's Clothing

Hawthorn Books, Inc.
Publishers
New York

WORDS IN SHEEP'S CLOTHING

2   3   4   5   6   7   8   9   10

The author wishes to thank *Modern Age* for permission to quote from previously published material.

Contents

71237

CHAPTER 1

Double-Speak in America

Some years ago my attention was called by a colleague in the field of sociology to a little German book that bore the attractive title *Aus dem Wörterbuch des Untermenschen*. Since the most current meaning of *Untermensch* is "gangster," "thug," I thought I was in for a session of German underworld slang. Actually, the author had used the term in its more etymological sense, that of "the subhuman, or somewhat less than human, being." It turned out to be a discussion of the gobbledygook of German bureaucrats, which seems to be in no way inferior to our own. It made just as fascinating reading as what I had at first expected. Here were terms, twisted out of their original meanings and made to serve, in a forced-labor chain gang, the purposes of political officialdom.

It occurred to me as I read that, although we have several similar works in English, dealing with Washington Choctaw and even with Officialese, its British equivalent, we still lack a comprehensive dictionary of terms that have undergone shifts of meaning by deliberate action on the part of groups with an axe to grind, until these hapless words have come to mean either the opposite of what they originally meant, or something so remote and confusing that one hesitates to use them.

Theodore Roosevelt called these "weasel words," and with good reason. He did not invent the term, which seems to have first appeared in an article by Stewart Chaplin published in *Century Magazine* in 1900. But he did popularize it in a speech made in St. Louis in 1916: "One of our defects as a nation is a tendency to use what have been called 'weasel words.' When a weasel sucks an egg the meat is sucked out of the egg; and if you use a 'weasel word' after another, there is nothing left of the other."

The weasel word does not necessarily have to be attached to another, however. The term can be legitimately extended to cover any word of which the semantics are deliberately changed or obscured to achieve a specific purpose, or which is used in a given context for the sole purpose of impressing and bamboozling the reader or hearer.

Weasel words are shifty, tricky, dishonest. A few, intentionally coined and put into circulation, may be compared to fake ten-dollar bills. But the majority are good old words, words that once enjoyed standing and respectability in the word community, but were made to stray from their straight and narrow path, lead a double life, and become thoroughly untrustworthy. These are rather in the nature of clipped coins, or debased currency, like the regular U.S. dollar that was once worth a hundred cents and is now down to forty cents or less in purchasing power.

Two examples that everyone is familiar with are "liberal" and "democracy." The first has been so debauched from what it once meant that today those who want to subject the individual to full government control call themselves "liberals," while those who still believe in individual freedom have been forced to describe themselves as "libertarians." "Democracy" as a word (but fortunately not as an institution) died when the Communists began to call their regimes "People's Democracies," on the plea that they represented government "for" the people rather than "by" the people.

Semantic change is as old as language itself. But most semantic changes occur accidentally ("silly": first "blessed," then "a blessed fool," finally a "fool" pure and simple; "surly": changed in spelling from an original "sirly," "one who acts like a sir, masterful," then "arrogant," ultimately "sullen"). The process of deliberate semantic change is largely modern. Still, there are historical examples: the adjective "cavalier," which meant "gallant" in 1641, "free and easy" in 1657, but by 1751 had become, by Roundhead influence, "haughty, supercilious, offensive"; "Tory": an Irish rebel in the seventeenth century, one who opposed the Exclusion Act designed to keep Catholics off the British throne in 1680, a mere Conservative in 1830, but also a supporter of the British Crown during the American Revolution; or the name of a movement like "Fronde," bestowed derisively by Cardinal Mazarin upon his opponents when he likened them to little boys throwing stones with slings, but quickly picked up by those same opponents as their title to fame and glory.

There are several kindred processes: that of coining words and putting them into circulation for the purpose of engendering whatever the propagandists consider desirable frames of mind; that of giving existing words prefixes and suffixes that turn them into objects of what the public relations agency wants to arouse, be it scorn or admiration; that of surrounding words with carefully selected modifiers having pleasant or unpleasant associations, so that even when the associated words are removed, the words themselves will evoke the feeling desired by the manipulators.

It is only partly true that most of these deliberate semantic changes occur in the realm of politics and administration. As we go over the rather large lists we have accumulated, with a view to bringing out a *Vocabulary of the Untermensch* of our own, we find that weasel words appear in all fields of human endeavor. There is the arty, pseudo-intellectual group, which ranges over the fields of painting, sculpture, music, and literature, particularly of the "modern" variety. There is the pseudo-scientific array, where physical scientists, psychologists, educators, anthropologists, even linguists, vie with one another. There is, of course, the bulky political-legal family out of which gobbledygook has been built. There is an entire made-to-order vocabulary of publicity, advertising, and commercialism, where the object is to sell the sizzle rather than the steak. There is a vocabulary of economics, one of sociology, particularly of the racial variety, one of journalism, one of labor relations, one of patriotism and military science, even one of sex. Full treatment of the subject calls for a book that will never be complete, because each year sees a bumper crop of new weasel words. Were weasel words an agricultural commodity, we would have more than enough to feed the hungry millions of India, Egypt, and other worthy recipients of our bounty.

Unfortunately, that is not the case. What we have instead is wheat for the threshing-floors of our dictionaries, and something to relish in the privacy of our studies, for as long as the privacy and the studies may endure. All we can do here is to offer a substantial sampling of what can be done to a language's vocabulary if one really sets his mind to it.

In exploring this entrancing field, we shall follow as scientific a procedure as we know how. Every word has a derivation and an etymological sense, which is sometimes surprisingly different from its present-day accepted meaning. The Concise Oxford Dictionary of 1932 gives us a clear picture of the word's first recorded appearance in English, and the evolution of its various acceptances. Sometimes, by comparing the Oxford Dictionary with an American dictionary, we can get an idea of the different things the same word means in the two major branches of the English language; but in these days of rapid communications and easy interchange, such differences are less important than you would think. Lastly, by comparing two editions of an American dictionary, say our old 1864 Webster's (printed in 1884) and the Third Edition of 1961, or the even more recent Random House Dictionary (1966), we can see what has been done to the word in recent times. How and by whom it has been done the dictionaries seldom say. But in the case of a good many words, we know from other sources, or can surmise. Seldom is the purpose impenetrable, where there is a purpose. It would be nice if we could suggest a remedy of the active kind, but the remedies that have been tried will not work. The only sure cure is total avoidance of the word that has undergone debasement. Treat it as you would a phony ten-dollar bill. Don't accept it, and don't pass it on.

In addition to individual terms that either have been coined to suit a purpose, or have been deliberately wrenched out of their traditional connotations into new twisted meanings that are often the reverse of the original, there are special semantic time-bombs that have been attached to combinations of words, the individual components of which are otherwise left free to retain their pristine innocence.

It is one of the merits of the more recent Merriam Webster Third Edition and the Random House Dictionary that they give recognition to word groups that were either ignored by older editions or (and this is more often the case) did not exist at the time of the compilation. There may be value in an examination of some of these combinations which changing times have brought to us.

In the matter of changing semantics of individual words, we can go deeply into the history and etymology of the words cited. This task is largely unnecessary in the case of word combinations, since with rare exceptions the semantic content of the constituent parts is unchanged. Historical examination will therefore be undertaken only when necessary.

The basic methodology is simple, and once it is illustrated, any reader so inclined may proceed on his own. There is lots of fun to be had with words, particularly weasel words.

In this work, we shall see words like "liberty" and "democracy" neutralized by appropriating them and applying them to systems that are basically slavery and absolutism; a word like "colonialism" invested with a disreputable aura by reminding Americans that they once suffered from "colonial" status; "profits" brought into disrepute by coupling them with "excessive," "bloated," "extortionate." Keep on repeating that the steeply progressive income tax is the "fairest" form of raising revenue, and people will swallow it and stand for it. Put a "non-violent" label on subversive activities, and you can justify even a riot.

Such is the power of words, in a society where reality no longer has meaning, and the word-symbol has become paramount.

CHAPTER 2

Words from Madison Avenue

Once upon a time there was a TV commercial that warned you of the dangers of "halitosis," and prescribed the remedy and safeguard. Then some Madison Avenue genius discovered that "halitosis" was much too learned a word for mass audiences, and suggested the more down-to-earth "bad breath" as a substitute. Still later, another advertiser decided to cannibalize the discarded word, in the same fashion that automobile mechanics cannibalize old wrecks in the junkyards to supply no longer available parts for old models. "This house has housitosis!" exclaimed the main character in a new commercial that offered a spray guaranteed to banish house odors forever.

"If headaches persist or recur frequently, see your doctor" ran the message for a preparation that would do away with occasional headaches. Then the wording changed: "If headaches hang on or keep coming back." "Persist" and "recur" were apparently also beyond the mass-audience pale.

A certain soap guarded you against "B.O.," a euphemistic abbreviation for "body odor." Now another preparation just "guards" you and your family (you can't leave your wife and children unprotected, you know!). And aren't you glad you use a third preparation, and don't you wish everybody did?

These episodes illustrate the nature and methods of the Madison Avenue language, the tongue of advertising. In many countries, weasel words and weasel wording are almost exclusively political. With us, they are at least as much com-

7

mercial, because we are a nation where consumption is at least as much at a premium as production.

Commercial advertising is very ancient. The first recorded sample of Latin, from about 500 B.C., is an inscription on a belt buckle that tells the reader, across twenty-five centuries, "Manius made me for Numerius," advertising both the long-dead manufacturer and the equally extinct customer for whom the article was made to order. The big vogue for advertising came in the nineteenth century. The French word for advertising is *réclame*, whose etymology goes back to Latin *re* and *clamo*, "to shout again." And the shouting is indeed done again and again and again, as any radio listener or television viewer can testify.

The techniques? Everything in the book. There is repetition *ad nauseam*, which is the very soul of propaganda. There is the use of special words meant to arouse special images. There is the adroit placing of carefully selected modifiers before equally selected nouns and verbs. Where a word that is desired does not exist, it is created. Grammar, usage, even pronunciation go by the board if necessary. Prefixes and suffixes are worked overtime. Above all, there are slogans, catchwords, phrases, sentences, ditties that are drummed into your ears until you have them fully memorized, whether you want to or not. No political propaganda bureau could do a better job with ideologies than our advertising agencies do with products.

It has been observed, however, that our advertising industry owes a fairly large part of its prominence to a political cause—the income tax, which makes it profitable and desirable for corporations that manufacture products to pour much of their excess profits into advertising, because otherwise "the government gets it." This is the real reason why advertising, in all its ramifications, is one of our biggest and most prosperous industries, and why our most prominent actors and actresses find it more profitable to appear on TV programs and commercials than on stage or screen. That is why "surveys" are constantly conducted to find out how many listen to whom and what at any given moment of the day or night. Here we get such weasel terms as "rating" and "Hooperating," final computerized sum totals that tell the advertiser what kind of program, or even what kind of commercial, draws the biggest mass audience. The commercial "survey" is very similar to the political "poll"; in fact, it is as often as not conducted by the same experts and methods. All of us are acquainted with the complaint, voiced by ourselves or our neighbors: "Why don't they ever ask *me*?" "Why don't they call *me* on the phone?" "Why don't they ring *my* doorbell?" But we know from political polls that something like 1,500 representative persons are supposed to give you an indication of how seventy million voters will vote on election day. "What are *my* chances of being polled?" asked a woman at a cocktail party of a poll director. "About the same as your chances of being struck by lightning," he unhesitatingly and truthfully replied.

This "scientific" sampling method, despite everything they tell you about mathematical and statistical accuracy and small chances of deviation, has come a cropper many times in political polls. One need only recall the demise of the old *Literary Digest* after it predicted Landon's victory over Roosevelt in 1936; Truman's upset victory over Dewey in 1948, contrary to poll predictions; and the fantastic preconvention gyrations of the 1968 polls, no two of which ever agreed, and no one of which remained consistent throughout. In political polls there is always a day of reckoning, Election Day. In the case of commercial polls and Hooperatings, who knows how many good programs have been discontinued and how many bad ones retained because the sampling was not broad enough or not sufficiently representative of the people the advertiser wanted to reach? A recent news item stated that the King Family program had been discontinued by reason of a computer error in the Hooperating. When the error was discovered, it was too late to rectify it.

At any rate, the field of radio and television advertising gives us many interesting words and expressions which show weasely features in varying amounts. There is the "live" (on TV or radio), which is sometimes opposed to the "pre-recorded" (or canned). There is the "prime time" (the early evening hours, when the largest number of viewers are supposed to be glued to their sets), which is reminiscent of "prime" beef. (One wonders, in fact, why the grading is not followed through; what is wrong with labeling the late evening hours as "choice"?) There is the agency "survey," as sacred a word in its own way as is "poll"; those who conduct the survey to determine what "the people" want become the high priests of an ultramodern cult. There is the "word from our sponsor," which seemed to grate on the ear of the viewer and was turned into a less pretentious and more laconic "message." Only a few program directors have the courage of their convictions, like Alfred Hitchcock, and call it, with the proper tone of scorn and loathing, "a commercial."

The program, as everybody knows, is only a pretext for the commercial "message"—everybody, that is, except the sponsors and their agencies. They do not realize that putting on a fine program is like leading a horse to water. Whether the horse drinks or not depends on the commercial. Some commercials are good and arouse a spirit of friendliness toward the product and its manufacturer. Others are unspeakably loud, blary, screechy, childish, moronic, stupid, and in bad taste. When this happens (and it happens far too often) the sponsor has spent his millions to arouse antagonism toward his product. Of course we know that tastes are not all alike, that one man's meat is another man's poison. All I can say is that when I'm bombarded with "It's not how long you make it" or confronted with the unspeakable character who throws his female companion out of his car after first retrieving his cigarettes, which she only wants to sample, all temptation to try those particular brands leaves me. And I am a confirmed smoker and willing to experiment.

The language of advertising comes at us in both spoken and written form. Several studies have been conducted to find out which are the most popular words among the advertisers. The results are even more inconclusive than the 1968 pre-convention polls. Here are two lists; both are top-heavy with adjectives, as one would expect; but no words coincide. One gives "glamour" (the sole noun); "chic"; "sociable"; "fashionable"; "perishable"; "free"; "guaranteed"; "jumbo"; "oversized"; "pre-owned"; "refreshing." The other features two nouns, "power" and "experience"; then it goes on to "chock-full"; "eye-catching"; "unbelievable"; "special"; "satisfying"; "amazing"; "whopping"; "first"; "ideal"; "long-lasting"; "sparkling", "better than ever"; "relaxing"; "timely"; "big"; "mild"; "top"; "exclusive"; "expensive." It is fairly obvious that the compilers of the two lists were in the habit of watching different programs, with different commercials.

The word that to us seems to hold an absolute lead (but this is a general impression, and not based on any scientific or statistical survey) is NEW, or better yet, N-E-W!!! Quite often, "new" is followed by "kind of." Another one that strikes us as high-frequency is "now" used as an adjective ("the now car"). Both words are commented on elsewhere; both are good old Anglo-Saxon three-letter words, and we are even indebted to the agencies for forcing us to discover that the use of "now" as an adjective goes back several centuries. At first we were shocked by "the now taste of Tab," but when we looked into it, we found the Oxford Dictionary offering samples from as far back as 1444, in the sense of "present," "existing" ("the now king," "the now judge"). Could our Madison Avenue agencies be guilty of research into Old and Middle English, we wondered? Could they be planning to bring other archaisms back to life? Or is all this purely coincidental? For what it may be worth, Random House, the most up-to-date of our comprehensive dictionaries, neither lists nor exemplifies the use of "now" as an adjective.

Other items in the two high-frequency lists lend them-

selves to comment. "Pre-owned" is described as the modern
euphemism for "second-hand." "Free" and "guaranteed" have
to be used guardedly, having been made the subjects of legal
proceedings and court decisions. Something cannot be called
"free," said the courts, if there is a financial condition attached
to your obtaining it; and "guaranteed" has to be specific of
what is guaranteed and for how long. Of "jumbo," a foreign
observer in our midst remarked that in America there are no
"small" eggs; only "medium," "large," "extra large," and
"jumbo." The word, incidentally, dates back to 1823 and
comes from "Mumbo Jumbo," described by the Oxford Dictionary as the name of an oversized West African divinity;
Webster's Third adds "jumboism," the American addiction to
the cult of bigness; but the Random House Dictionary dis-
putes this derivation, and traces "jumbo" back to the name of
one of Barnum's elephants, derived from Swahili *jumbe*,
"chief"; while Partridge suggests the possibility of derivation
from Congolese *nzombo*, "python." As with the varieties of
eggs mentioned by our foreign observer, you pay your money
and take your choice.

The coining of trade names is a fairly ancient practice, and
even before Madison Avenue existed as an institution, there
were always enough publicity-minded individuals on hand to
coin such catchy names as "Kodak," "sanforized," and "cello-
phane." (The last, going back to 1921, is an ingenious blend
of "cellulose" and "diaphane," the two main ingredients.)
There is no question that some of the coinages are both
legitimate and clever. "Homemaker," for instance, was created
to get away from the drudgery connotations of "housewife."
"Wedding white" (what lovely imagery!), "planned community" (this is simply a real-estate development), "slim-
nastics" (gymnastics that slim you down), "problem skin"
(this does away with "eczema," "psoryasis," and other loath-
some names of skin diseases) are samples. Coinages of the
type of "power-pak" are a dime a dozen; they sound so

dynamic and go-go-ish! "Poorthink" was thought up by the agencies to convince businessmen, who generally need no convincing, that when they travel on a tax-deductible expense account they should by all means use the most, not the least expensive accommodations. The "Oldsmobile" is converted into a "Youngmobile" so that it may appeal to all those who "think young" and are now affluent by reason of the generous allowances their hard-working parents bestow upon them.

"Blah" is described as a semi-interjection that arose in the United States around 1921 to betoken meaningless talk ("And then he went on, blah, blah, blah"). But an ingenious agency managed to turn it into the name of a common complaint, the "Monday morning blahs," depicted on the screen as common to New York, London, Moscow, New Delhi, and Hong Kong, and for which there is, of course, a sure cure. In the visual description that accompanies the commercial it is implied, though not expressly stated, that the "blahs" condition is brought about by overindulgence during the weekend. But does the day of rest, with its subsequent and resultant blahs, coincide in all these widely separated parts of the world? The Moslems celebrate Friday, the Hindus Thursday. Should we not therefore eliminate that "Monday morning" from our blahs?

The world of advertising has created "gracious living," where "gracious" has lost its original content of "kind," "benignant," especially in a religious sense, and has brazenly acquired that of "characterized by taste, wealth, luxury, comfort." Another favorite phrase, "the good life," once a life of virtue, led in accord with moral or religious precepts, is now one marked by "a high standard of living" and abounding in "material comforts and luxuries." A third but little-used meaning of "the good life" is one "characterized by the harmonious, many-sided development of the individual," but this is largely lost in the materialistic shuffle for the "good" things of life.

Another sample of the linguistic creativity of the advertising world comes from the Washington, D.C., area, into which many corporate giants have been expanding their research and pouring their facilities and personnel. The highways of the area are reportedly studded with signs bearing such exotic names as "Orbit Industries," "Galaxy," "Systemetrics," "Versitron," "Sensonics," "Geonautics," "Multronics," "Adaptronics," "Cosmic," "Exotech," "Longetronics," "Presearch," and "Technigraphics."

It is small wonder that a columnist supplies us with a list of automobile advertising terms, some of which may even be authentic: "motoramic," "metal-in-motion," "hyfire," "trigger-torque power," "angle-poised ride," "speed trigger drive," "turbo-action sparkplugs." The sizzle sounds better than the steak tastes.

The slogans of the advertising world are designed to sell the product. Almost as often, they are designed to run down the competition. Forgive the paraphrasing and consider these familiar and very thinly disguised battle flags: "Greasy kid stuff!" "25% fewer cavities!" (fewer than what?) "I'd rather switch than fight!" "There's nothing like a Shark!" "Any coffee is reheatable if you don't boil it!"

Then there are those that seem to call for a rounding out, or a slight modification: "Put a tiger in your tank!" (But what's the good if you have a jackass at the wheel?) "Who is the junkman? It could be you!" "Eye to eye; halitosis to halitosis!" "For those who think old!" "Have a cow-dung cigarette!" "It's a green tornado!" "The filter's in the charcoal!" "We must be doing something wrong!" "Leave it to Blisterine!" "Come on over; you'll be sorry you did!" "Now we're a five-toothpaste family again!"

There are the ones that challenge your manhood: "Are you man enough to try it?" "Come on, all you tigers!" "You're a man, aren't you?" "Take it all off!" "Come alive! You're in the switched-on generation!"

This could go on and on, but what would be the use? One final question: if *El Exigente* is as *exigente* as he claims to be, why doesn't he ever shake his head and say no? What would happen to him if he did? Would they shoot him? Run him out of town? Put him to hard labor for life picking inferior coffee beans? He had better nod approval and set the fireworks going and the band playing!

The language of advertising has been accused of bringing corruption to the common English tongue. Actually, this doesn't happen too often. If anything, it brings standardization of a not too objectionable type, though on the colloquial level, because the tongue of coast-to-coast commercials must be accessible to all localities within our land, and cannot afford to burden itself with localisms.

A few points of grammar are violated, but only in response to widespread practices among the speakers ("like a cigarette should"; "Us Tareyton smokers would rather fight than switch"). The Madison Avenue innovation that should perhaps arouse the greatest amount of comment, because it sets its own usage, consists of taking nouns, treating them as adjectives, and endowing them with comparative and superlative forms ("coffee-er coffee"; "it's the peanuttiest"; "the macaroniest"). In the general language of advertising we find such distortions as "chaise lounge" for *chaise longue* (here the justification is that customers tend to pronounce it that way, and anyhow, it is appropriate for lounging), and the new adjective "flammable," frankly and pragmatically justified on the ground that the *in-* of "inflammable" may easily be misunderstood as a negative prefix meaning "not" rather than an intensive prefix.

More than any other linguistic field, advertising is given to the use and expansion of prefixes and suffixes. There is the superabundant use of *super-*. There is a use of *-ex* in trade names ("Kleenex," "Windex") that is said to be influenced by the *ex-* of "excellent." There is the very modern application of *un-* to products ("the Uncola"), but this expansion of *un-* appears in many other fields. There is the expansion of *-rama* or *-orama* ("motorama") for spectacles; of *-cade* for spectacles in motion ("aquacade," "motorcade"); of *-matic* for mechanical appliances ("hydromatic"); of *-eria* for places where certain goods or services may be procured ("valeteria," "booketeria"). Here we have a transfer of a suffix from an original word which happened to be in widespread use ("panorama," "cavalcade," "automatic," "cafeteria"; the last is described by the Oxford Dictionary as having first appeared in 1839, in the United States, as a borrowing from Spanish). The *-ique* of French *boutique* has lately been seized upon to form such chic creations as "footique" and "bootique" for milady's shoe stores.

In summary, the language of advertising may be described as being among the most frankly and openly weasely of all. But then its purpose is clearly stated, and we should not really mind if those who have something to sell present it in what is to them (not necessarily to us) the most linguistically attractive form possible.

We have seen that the language of advertising goes all the way back to the early Romans of the fifth century B.C. But those same Romans also supplied us with a linguistic safeguard against commercial wiles: *Caveat emptor*, "Let the buyer beware!"

CHAPTER 3

What Makes a Picture Great?

The tongue of stage and screen has many points of contact with the Madison Avenue language, even though it stems from Broadway and Hollywood. Many terms are held in common by the two arts, others are peculiar to the one or the other.

"Angel," "Rialto," "on the road," "Borsht circuit," pertain to the living stage. "Tin Pan Alley" belongs to popular music, or, at the most, to musical comedy; but since the latter as often as not passes on to the screen, there is a common link. Terms of glowing publicity can easily be applied to either: "hit," or better yet, "smash hit"; "classic"; "stark drama."

Some of these words are weasely only by remote implication. "Angel," for example, is a term reserved for the financial backer of a stage production. The word, first used in English in a religious sense, stems from Greek *angelos*, "messenger." Christianity appropriates it and makes it a "messenger of God." Not until 1592 was the word figuratively applied to a person. Its modern Broadway use is quite recent, as attested by the fact that the Oxford Dictionary does not define it as having that connotation. But our American dictionaries do, and Webster's Third adds the final note whereby it is turned into a mild weasel word: any rich fool who can be hoodwinked into pouring money into a dubious enterprise.

"Rialto" is the ancient bridge over the Grand Canal in Venice, where business used to be transacted in the days of the Doges. The Italian name means a "rise," something raised, and the Rialto arches up over the canal, in keeping with its name. It comes into English with the meaning of "market" or "exchange" in 1897 (in fact Wall Street is sometimes also called "the Rialto"), and again the Oxford Dictionary gives it only in that sense. But our American dictionaries carry the meaning on to a "theatrical district," which is only in part justified by the fact that some theaters exist in the vicinity of the Venetian bridge.

"On the road" is, in a sense, literal. Again, the Oxford Dictionary fails to mention it in the American sense of "on a theatrical tour." Our American works give the impression that it was used for traveling salesmen before it got to be applied to theater circuits. The "Borsht circuit" is a purely American expression indicating summer theater presentations held in the Jewish Catskill resorts, where that ancient and popular Slavic beet-and-sour-cream soup is consumed in large quantities. Similarly, "Tin Pan Alley" is described only in the American dictionaries as the New York City district where publishers of popular music carry on their trade. (Wentworth and Flexner locate the area as between 48th and 52nd Streets, near Seventh Avenue.)

The stage has also given us the name of that French-born institution, the "claque," which entered English in 1864 and betokens a group of hired people who sprinkle themselves among theater audiences and lead insincere applause. A producer once said that a "clique" is to a "claque" as an ordinary holdup is to Murder, Incorporated.

More recent terms of stage, screen, and television are the "Oscar" and the "Tony." These are the statuettes bestowed upon Academy and Theatre Wing award winners. The first got its name because an Academy secretary remarked that the figure reminded her of her uncle Oscar, while the second was named after the popular actress Antoinette Perry, who had been nicknamed "Tony." The word had been in British use since 1784 in the sense of "simpleton," but the would-be coiners did not know that. "Femcee" is another recently coined term for a female master of ceremonies—or should we say "Mistress of Ceremonies"? Only Webster's Third recognizes it. Then there is "star," used in connection with the theater since 1824, its superlative "superstar," and its derivative "starlet," for a young movie actress who is still training for major roles; but this is a very recent use for a word that first appears in English in 1830, and for a long time carried the meanings of "small star," "a variety of flower," and "a variety of starfish."

The true weasel words of stage and screen are the ones used in publicity, to create an image and draw paying customers, and the ones coined in derision, generally by the news media, but quite often by the industry itself.

Typical of the first are the nouns "epic" and "saga," "talent" and "celebrity," "hit" and "classic"; the adjectives "award-winning," "colossal," "spectacular," "gorgeous," "fabulous." The latter category includes the slightly contemptuous "Western," "Eastern," "soap opera" and "horse opera," "whodunit" and "mystery" (but the last two are also applied to books); old formations in -*eroo* ("twisteroo," switcheroo," "stinkeroo"); the ultramodern "minicast," to describe a very small cast. (Some very modern plays and films are conducted with only two people in the cast, both usually in the same bed at the same time.)

The "hit" of "smash hit" has been in use in the sense of "something successful" since 1915, but the Oxford Dictionary does not list it in the sense of a theatrical success, while the American dictionaries do. "Classic" ("stage" or "screen," but more usually the latter) is a word that has drawn much criticism. It first appears in English in 1613, in the sense of a book that is used in classes; this in effect means that at first only classical works were classics. The term was gradually extended by 1711 to any deserving work of literature. Our modern dictionaries accept it in a musical and artistic as well as literary sense; but a *New York Times* editorial writer deplores the fact that eight out of ten pictures are hailed as "screen classics," and thinks we should go back to using the term exclusively for books.

"Epic" used as a noun goes back to 1589. The original Greek *epos* meant narrative poetry, usually of the unwritten, traditional variety. Our modern dictionaries carry it on to any form of heroic composition, and Webster's Third specifically accepts it for prose narrative and for screen offerings. It, too, is occasionally overused. "Saga," the last of our laudatory nouns, is an old Norse word for Icelandic epic poems. With an assist from German use, it penetrates English in 1709, is applied to any mythological or historical narrative of epic proportions by 1864, and acquires, in the early 1900s, the meaning of a protracted, leisurely chronicle dealing with an entire family (as in Galsworthy's *Forsyte Saga*). Its application to screen offerings does not seem warranted, save in special cases.

Two vastly overused words in stage and screen publicity are "celebrity" and "talent." The first, however, has received from journalistic use an extension that carries it far beyond either stage or screen. It is derived from Latin *celeber*, "famous," and has been used in English from 1600 on, but only in the abstract sense of "the state of being celebrated." In its present nightclub sense of "a celebrated person" it has been in use only since 1849. The 1961 Webster's defined it in this acceptance as "one popularly honored for some signal achievement." Our objection is not to the semantic shift, but only to the application of the word, in gossip columns, to people who have no claim to fame save the fact that they put in an appearance every night at El Morocco or whatever nightery may have replaced the Stork Club. For them, we should like to suggest the coinage of "notorieties" to replace "celebrities."

"Talent" is another overworked word. Originally it meant "balance," then the object weighed, then a unit of both weight and money. It is suggested that the use of the talents in the New Testament parable may have led to the new meaning of "abilities, powers, gifts, natural endowments," thought of at first, perhaps, as a divine trust. "Superior intellectual ability," "natural capacity" appear in other definitions. The weight-and-money meaning goes all the way back to Anglo-Saxon, the power-of-the-mind meaning back to Middle English. There is a curious British acceptance of "talent," as applied to an individual, to describe a backer of horses (not a bookmaker). The modern American acceptance does not differ in kind, but only in degree, from the older, with "talent" applied in describing anyone who can lift his voice or his feet, whether or not he (or she) can really sing or dance. It has therefore degenerated into a press-agent word; in proof whereof we advance the 1961 Webster's definition of a "talent scout" as one who goes out and looks, among other things, for oil dealers and football players.

Among our adjectives of praise, "award-winning" is self-explanatory, and all we can ask of those who use it is that it be authentic. "Spectacular" is, etymologically, self-defeating, because *spectaculum* is anything you look at, and *specto* simply means "to look upon." "Colossal" is suspected by many of having received a boost from the German *kolossal* in use among many of our German-born film directors, though the word has been in English use since 1712. "Gorgeous," used in English since 1495, is of somewhat mysterious derivation. Some authorities derive it from the name of Gorgias, a Greek rhetorician who was also a fashion arbiter; others from French *gorgias*, "neckerchief," but also "elegant attire," which goes back to *gorge*, "throat." At any rate, "gorgeous" is used in many other fields besides stage and screen.

A true weasel word is "fabulous," which according to theatrical tradition was first applied by a press agent to Billy Rose. It comes from Latin *fabula*, "fairy tale," which in turn goes back to the root of *fari*, "to speak." In English it has been in use since 1546, but in the sense of "feigned, fictitious, like a fable, especially in exaggeration, astounding"; the meaning "incredible" is added in 1609. These connotations continue unbroken in our 1884 Webster's. But something new has been added by the 1961 version: "outstanding or remarkable, especially in some acceptable or pleasing quality." This, of course, is the Hollywood and Madison Avenue acceptance in which one speaks of a fabulous production, a fabulous producer, a fabulous product. As in the case of "culture" used anthropologically, we come close to a reversal of meaning, with the word continuing in existence in two almost opposite acceptances. It seems a good word to avoid. The ironic "fantabulous," by the way, is deemed unworthy of inclusion in any of our dictionaries.

Among words of derision and implied condemnation, particularly for films, are terms like "cliff-hanger" for those pictures that leave the heroine literally or metaphorically hanging from a cliff, to be rescued in next week's episode; "Western," which the Oxford Dictionary does not apply to films, but which both Webster's Third and the Random House Dictionary abundantly describe in that connotation, along with its synonyms, "horse opera," "oater," "sage-brusher," and "they-went-thatawayer." (The last, of course, is derived from the reply given to the leader of the posse by eyewitnesses to the bank robbery.) "Spaghetti Western" and "Sukiyaki Western" are terms applied to cheap Westerns produced in Italy and Japan. On the analogy of "Western," Hollywood coined "Eastern" to describe those spectacular spectacles which feature the sands of the Sahara or Gobi instead of those of Arizona or Nevada, and scimitars instead of six-shooters. But this usage is recognized by none of our dictionaries.

The "soap opera" is really a specialty of radio and television. It gets its name from the fact that at first it was overwhelmingly sponsored by soap manufacturers, and both American dictionaries describe it as running in a series, preferably five days a week, dealing with the problems, troubles, and tribulations of a group, preferably a family, and characterized by effusive sentimentality, sometimes to the point of becoming a "tear-jerker."

The "mystery" and "whodunit" are shared by stage and screen with the field of literature. Both terms are recent. "Whodunit" is said to have been coined in 1930 by Donald Gordon, who used it in *American News of Books*. Webster's Third describes the term as "substandard" (quite an admission for this dictionary); the Random House Dictionary lists it as merely "informal" or "jocular." Interesting is the fact that other languages often use for "whodunit" the color of the jacket or cover (Italian *romanzo giallo*, "yellow novel," French *roman noir*, "black novel," side by side with *roman policier*, "detective novel"). There is no semantic connection between the medieval "mystery play" and the modern mystery story or film. In the first, the outcome was known in advance by the audience; in the second, the viewer or reader is invited, or even challenged, to figure out "who done it" before he reaches the end.

There is in the field one suffix which may be described as derogatory, and that is the *-eroo* of "twisteroo," "stinkeroo," "puncheroo," etc. The base word which supplies the analogical force seems to be "buckaroo," a western U.S. modification of Spanish *vaquero*, "cowboy," with an assist from "buck" and a shift of stress from the penult to the last syllable. How and why the extension came about is not clear. The dictionaries are of no help, save for the root words. "Twister," however, goes all the way back to 1579, and is a popular U.S. term for "tornado," while "stinker," applied to a person, goes back to 1607.

CHAPTER 4

The Arts and the Arty

The life of the Intellectual Cocktail Party is definitely based on an argot which has to be combined with the appropriate subject matter—music, art (preferably modern), the dance, the theater, the cinema, literature.

Various writers have repeatedly given us lists of recommended words and phrases, whose chief merit is that they mark the speaker as an esthete and connoisseur and set him apart from the lowly crowd of baseball fans and local politicians.

Do these words and phrases qualify as weasel words? Some are used in legitimate connotations, others are technical terms which would be missed if they were not available, and still others belong to the overrefined, polysyllabic segment of the vocabulary. Some are low-down to the point of being qualified as slang in the dictionaries that make a distinction between standard and substandard language. Some are surprisingly ancient, others surprisingly modern.

Their point of contact lies in the fact that they are designed to impress the hearer and make him think the speaker is an expert in the artistic specialty under discussion. There is among them plenty of overlapping with other fields than the purely artistic. Where does art end and philosophy (or psychology, or even politics) begin? A few prefixes and suffixes (*neo-*, *non-*, *-ism*) illustrate the problem. "Neo-sensorialism" runs side by side with "neo-Fascism," "non-objective" and "non-representational" with "non-academic" and "non-democratic."

Nevertheless, it is possible to isolate a number of words and offer a cross-section of what R. G. Saisselin, writing in *The New York Times*, once described as "the Vocabulary of the Arts." He pointed out, to be sure, that the follower of the arts has no alphabet, creates his own rules, thereby making communication difficult, and that while the artist often jibbers, his critic just as often jabbers.

Saisselin's samples are for the most part of the long-established, spread-out variety. "Gripping" ("when using, ask yourself where it grips and whether you really enjoy being gripped") goes back to Anglo-Saxon, though only in 1891, according to the Oxford Dictionary, does it turn figurative in the sense of "taking hold on the mind or emotions."

"Experience" ("an unfortunate term") started its artistic career with an unreadable book that had a catchy title, *Art as Experience*. An artist or writer must "experience life" to be truly great. This gives artists and writers no credit for imagination, says Saisselin; Homer and Tolstoy "experienced" neither Troy nor Borodino. But "experience," in addition to having a wealth of non-artistic uses, goes back to Middle English. People began to "experience religion" in 1674.

"Interesting" (1768, in the sense of "exciting interest"), "immediate" (sixteenth century), "provocative" (1621 in the sense of "exciting appetite or lust," and used earlier in Middle English in the sense of "aphrodisiac"), "sublime" (1586), "sincere," and "beautiful" are all words that have long histories and numerous applications, but as overapplied in the artistic field, they have largely lost their meanings.

For "uninhibited," which is offered as a substitute for "sincere," we have a problem. It does not appear in the 1932 Oxford Dictionary, though "inhibit" goes back to 1460. Webster's Third gives it only in the sense of "boisterously informal." The later Random House Dictionary defines it as "unconstrained, shocking, not restrained by social conventions." Its application to a work of art seems a doubtful recommendation.

Three terms in the list present unusual features. One is "Libidinal Trinity," offered as a replacement for "Muses," which I have been unable to find anywhere else. In fact, even "libidinal" fails to appear in the 1932 Oxford Dictionary.

Another is "thereness," which Saisselin offers as a substitute for the imported *Dasein* and equates to "immediate," a term to be used, not overused, in conjunction with what is exciting, brutal, tough, hard, raw. "Thereness" (1674) is described as rare in the Oxford Dictionary, which contrasts it to "hereness." Webster's Third defines it as "real existence, the quality of being there, not here." The Random House Dictionary, the most modern of our dictionaries, strangely overlooks it. *Dasein* itself is defined by Webster's Third as "in existentialism, factual reality or existence within the spatiotemporal realm," by the Random House Dictionary as "the sensation of existence with full awareness of the conditions of one's existence." Not only do these words qualify for weasel status; they are even reminiscent of an old vaudeville line: "Was you there, Charlie?"

"Empathy" crosses boundaries, especially the one bordering on psychology. Saisselin calls it a "good" word; since "feeling" is out, "empathy" has been mobilized to save non-objective, impressionistic, and abstract painting generally from the critical reason; old ladies may "feel" with Renoir, but we must empathize with de Kooning. The first appearance of the word was in 1912, and it is definitely a translation of the German *Einfühlung*. The Oxford Dictionary speaks of "projecting one's personality into and thus understanding the object of our contemplation." Webster's Third calls it "reading one's mind into an artistic object," or the "vicarious experience of another's feelings." The Random House Dictionary calls it "attributing to an object feelings which are in oneself." No matter how you slice "empathy," it exudes a faint weasely smell.

Our own list of artistic words that may feature weasely

qualities includes "modern" (or "contemporary"), "non-objective" (or "non-representational"); "abstract"; "creative"; "conceptual"; "decadent" (but this one has political overtones); "pragmatic" (this word cuts across many boundaries); "functional"; "three-dimensional"; "dichotomy" (usually preceded by "insoluble"; but again a word that is used in many other fields); "ambivalent" (at least as much psychological as artistic); "perceptive"; "evocative"; "free-flowing"; "linear"; "fluid"; "sculptured"; "intuitive"; "organic"; names of movements ("plasticism," "surrealism," "sensorialism," "existentialism"); expressions like "stream of consciousness"; all-purpose words like "ethos" and "esthetic"; foreign borrowings like *Kitsch, succès d'estime, un je ne sais quoi, mystique.*

Some of these words go pretty far back in the history of the language. "Abstract," for example, first appears in 1542, "pragmatic" in 1587, "dichotomy" in 1610, "functional" in 1611. On the other hand, "conceptual" first appears in 1834, "decadent" in 1837. "Non-objective" and "non-representational" do not appear in the Oxford Dictionary, though our more recent American dictionaries define them as "representing no concrete object of nature." "Kinesthetic," which likewise fails to appear in the 1932 British work, is given by Webster's Third as "involving bodily reaction, motor memory," and by the Random House Dictionary as "involving the sensation of movement." "Ambivalent," listed by the Oxford Dictionary as first appearing in 1921, is defined by Webster's Third as "having contradictory reactions," and by the Random House Dictionary as "having positive and negative feelings toward the same person." Only "plasticity" appears in the Oxford Dictionary and the Random House Dictionary, but Webster's Third gives us "plasticism" in the sense of the "theory of plastic art." "Surrealism" does not appear till 1927, according to the Oxford Dictionary; in art, it "represents and interprets the phenomena of dreams"; but Webster's Third calls it "fantastic, incongruous imagery achieved by unnatural combinations." While only the adjective form "sensorial" (1768) is given by our dictionaries, a definition that has come to me from other sources defines "sensorialism" as a claim that nothing is valid except experience of the senses, with sexual experience as the most intense and valid. "Existential" is from 1693, but "existentialism" (1944) is defined by the Random House Dictionary as "man's responsibility for shaping his own nature." The "stream of consciousness," which does not appear in the Oxford Dictionary, is defined in Webster's Third as "individual conscious experience coming in a series," and by the Random House Dictionary as a "style of writing involving random thoughts or perceptions, with no regard for logical expression, the rules of syntax, or levels of reality."

Among our foreign borrowings, *Kitsch*, though not given by the 1932 Oxford Dictionary, is exemplified in Webster's Third from 1907, identified as coming from a German dialect form, and given the meaning of "something scraped together." *Mystique*, a complex of legendary qualities woven around a person or institution, has been with us only since 1951.

The double definition of "ethos" given by the Random House Dictionary is surprising. On the one hand, it is the "fundamental characteristics of a culture, the underlying sentiments and dominant assumptions of a group"; on the other, it is the "moral element that determines the individual's actions rather than his thoughts or emotions." This would seem to imply that while the group is authorized to behave traditionally and emotionally, the individual is not.

"Modern," in artistic parlance, has two different interpretations. According to the U.S. Customs, "modern art" is anything produced after 1830 ("antique" is the opposite in this sense); but in its more general and "modern" acceptance, it is defined by Webster's Third and the Random House Dictionary as "contemporary, breaking with tradition, showing creative originality." Perhaps this is a good word to avoid.

Enough has probably been said to indicate that the more learned division of the vocabulary of art can on occasion be confusing and lend itself to massive misunderstandings. What of the more popular and slangy contingent of art words?

Here our list contains items with political overtones, such as "avant-garde" and "underground," older coinages like "middlebrow," more recent ones like "popendipity," based in turn on "pop," "pops," and perhaps "op." There are the delightful if mysterious "camp" and "happening," strange uses of common words ("in," "far out," "with it," "now" used as an adjective, "turned on," "bag"). Then there is the "action" whose whereabouts baffle us.

"Avant-garde," which the Oxford Dictionary does not list, comes, of course, from the French. Is it a vanguard or only a scouting patrol, ready to scurry back at the first sign of opposition? Is its mission, like that of the "Underground" (discussed more fully in Chapter 18), merely to bait, irritate, and distress the philistines? Webster's Third defines "avant-garde" as "original, unorthodox, untraditional, extremist, bizarre, arty, affected." To this list, the Random House Dictionary adds the concept of "employing experimental methods," which is quite an understatement.

"Middlebrow" is non-apparent in the Oxford Dictionary. Our American dictionaries define it as "moderately, not highly, cultivated." They equate a "middlebrow" with a philistine, one who has intellectual pretensions, but dislikes the original and unconventional. A middlebrow is the man in the middle between a highbrow and a lowbrow.

"Op," which does not appear in the Oxford Dictionary, is defined by the Random House Dictionary as a "style of abstract art with optical illusions." Its only connection with "pop" seems to be in the rhyme. "Pop" surprises us by appearing in the Oxford Dictionary, and being dated as far back as 1862, with the explanation that it is "short for popular concert." Then it gets crossed with Horace Walpole's "serendipity" of 1754 (the three good princes of Serendip, or

Sindhalawipa, or Ceylon, who in their travels enjoyed the blessing of finding pleasant things they were not looking for), and gives rise to "popendipity," presumably the ability to discover popular music which one is not seeking.

"Camp" is a real mystery word. In its more normal acceptances it goes back to 1528; but the Oxford Dictionary also lists a 1713 occurrence from the northern English dialects to denote a pile of potatoes or turnips covered over with straw and earth and left out in the open for winter storage. The Oxford Dictionary makes no mention of the up-to-date arty usage, which apparently had not yet arisen in 1932, or even in 1950. The Random House Dictionary defines "camp" as "artificiality" or "ostentation," with sinister overtones that have to do with brothels and meeting places for homosexuals. Richard Lingeman, writing in *The New York Times*, includes "camp" in his vocabulary of "Popspeak," defining it as a "cultural license, authenticated by *Partisan Review*, enabling you to like things which you were told were trashy when you were a child." Elsewhere, "camp" has been defined as "acceptance of the odd as artistic" and "conscious defense of excessive mannerisms," with the creation of a concomitant adjective, "campy" (though "camp" itself may be used as an adjective), and an opposite, "stoop" (could this be an abbreviation of "stupid"?), somebody or something who or which is not "camp." Luckily, the whole caboodle seems to be on its way out.

"Happening," on the contrary, is spreading to other countries (French *le happening*, *un happening*, Etiemble's fulminations against *le Franglais* to the contrary notwithstanding). In its normal sense of "event," "occurrence," the Oxford Dictionary traces it back to 1581, and it can be traced back still farther to Middle English and even Old Norse (*happ*, "chance," "good luck"). The modern arty use is fully described in the Random House Dictionary: "dramatic performance, particularly if it involves audience participation and the presentation of discontinuous events." Lingeman satirically extends it to cover individuals whose activity elicits pleasant surprise, "nowness," and charm. He seems inclined to trace it to the phrase "What's happening?" and defines it as "anything a journalist, editor, or copywriter wants to call to your attention." The past of "happening" is "happened," as in "Whatever happened to Baby Jane?"

"In," the phrase "to be in," is claimed by some to have originated in Britain ("In London, the off-season is definitely in"). The Oxford Dictionary informs us that it appears as far back as 1599 as an adjective connected with a noun by a hyphen ("in-brother," "in-patient"). The "ins" in the sense of "the party in power" starts in 1764, and as "the side that is up in games" in 1862. Our American dictionaries describe its current use as "to be in a position of assured success, in vogue, in style." "Far out," on the other hand, is given only by the Random House Dictionary in the sense of "unconventional, offbeat." "With it" ("to be with it," "to get with it") is surprisingly called "slangy" by Webster's Third, and its definition is another slang phrase, "to be on the beam." The Random House Dictionary more sedately defines it as "to be attentive, alert, appreciative, particularly of jazz." There seems to be no connection with an older if equally slangy use of "it" in the sense of "sex appeal" ("The It Girl").

"Now" used as an adjective cuts across the boundaries of the language of advertising ("the now car"; see p. 11 for its surprisingly ancient lineage). Lingeman applies it to persons as well as objects, and gives its opposite as "not-now," with such examples as Lyndon Johnson, Bud Collier, and Johnny Carson, who are said to have a "minimum corpo-reality, but little else."

"Super," without hyphen, is another word that is shuttled back and forth across the Atlantic, like a tennis ball. The Oxford Dictionary presents its first appearance in 1833 as a trade term, meaning "of fine grade." In present-day British usage, it often appears as an exclamation of approval ("Super, old boy!").

"Bag," in its normal meanings, goes back to Middle English and Old Norse. The Random House Dictionary also defines it as a "style of jazz," and Lingeman, seemingly farther in the van, reports its use as "a particular, limited, enclosed, yet liberating style of life or art, into and out of which the hip slip easily." We might add that in this sense it seems almost equivalent to "thing" ("Do your own thing!").

"Turned on," for a water tap or radio, is common to all our dictionaries. The Random House Dictionary adds another ominous note, "to start taking narcotics, or induce another to take them." This is the acceptance favored by Lingeman, who after describing an "acutely, wholly aware state of mind in which one can truly appreciate beauty and the meaning of life," goes on to "bombed out of your mind by some drug."

"The Action" ("where the action is") is equated by Webster's Third to "event." It is used in the gambling and betting world, from which it seemingly spread. Whether or not it is linked to its use as a "significant part of a religious ceremony," such as the Canon of the Mass, is obscure.

This cross-section on the language of the arts and the arty would be incomplete without a reference to an article J. Donald Adams wrote for *The New York Times* concerning the use, or non-use, that most modern poets and some modern writers make of punctuation. Many, he says, omit punctuation altogether. Others pin their faith on an unpredictable use of the colon, which he surmises indicates that the poet is catching his breath. Still others, like José García Villa, punctuate every word with a comma. He goes on to deplore the use of quotes to emphasize or qualify meaning ("liberal," "lady," indicating that to the writer the subject of the discussion is not a liberal and not a lady). All this began, he concludes, with the antics of Joyce and the clowning of Gertrude Stein, which seems plausible enough.

This misuse of the guide-lines of punctuation leads to the obliteration or obfuscation of meaning, and thus qualifies as a weasel practice.

CHAPTER 5

Debs, Mods, and Hippies

The late writer and columnist Robert Ruark once composed a column in which he protested volubly against being addressed as "honey," "sweetie," and "dear heart"; described as a "living doll"; and answered with such expressions as "all rightie" and "natch."

Although he blamed the "sweetie" routine on English actors who had brought it to America in the early Somerset Maugham epoch, it was pretty obvious that his real objection was to a he-man like himself being described and addressed in a feminine vocabulary. All the villainous characters in his piece were women and girls.

I will admit that I myself felt very strange when I called up my bank to report an error, and the lady bookkeeper, who had vainly been trying to trace the shortage for hours, thanked me effusively and concluded with "You're a doll!" This noun, as I discovered later, stems from 1560, when it was first used as a pet nickname for Dorothy, which Ruark and I obviously were not; then, by 1891, it got to be applied to any pretty but silly woman. It reached its full vogue by 1920 and finally got to be handed out as a sort of left-handed bonus to our masculine sex around 1940. Most of us still like "tall, dark, and handsome" much better.

One form of feminine address Ruark forgot to mention, though it was in full use at the time, was "darling," or, as actresses born in the South or in Hungary pronounce it, "dahling" or "dahlink." Another is "Hi, love!" What women

33

use among themselves is their own business, but must they inflict it on us?

It has long been known that Japanese is not the only language where there is a special feminine vocabulary that men may not, dare not, and will not use. Take this list, mostly of articles of attire, which display one or both of two important linguistic characteristics, abbreviation and what may be described as a feminine diminutive suffix: "hanky," "panties," "undies," "nappies," "scanties," "nightie." What man would dare to use them? "Nappies" is mainly British nursery colloquial for babies' napkins, or, as we would call them, diapers; still, it goes back to 1499. "Hanky" for "hand-kerchief" is suspected of being influenced by "hanky-panky," which goes back to 1841; its use as a feminine abbreviation for "handkerchief" has been traced back to 1895; the full word, by the way, is a piece of linguistic nonsense; its base form is "kerchief," which goes back to Old French *couvre-chief*, "cover-head"; a "hand-cover-head" does not make much sense. "Panties" has been traced back to 1846, but its real use begins in the 1920s; it is described as short, abbreviated pants worn by women and children (men, as everyone knows, wear shorts, not panties). "Scanties" first appears in 1874 as "scanty trowsers"; the "trowsers" are then dropped, and the adjective becomes a plural noun, on the analogy of "panties"; Webster's Third describes it as abbreviated panties for women, the Random House Dictionary as extremely short panties. "Undies" seemingly stems from 1918, and replaces a previously used "frillies"; it is obviously an abbreviation of "underwear," and the Random House Dictionary, but not Webster's Third, describes it as underwear designed for women and children. "Nightie" begins its career in 1895; the Random House Dictionary describes it as informal for "nightgown," while Webster's Third goes on to define it as used only for women's and children's nightgowns. There is some doubt as to whether another feminine expression, "nightie-night," is connected with it.

Two more supposedly feminine vocabulary items are "unmentionables" and "hair-do." The former was much in use between 1830 and 1900 for "trousers," then became obsolete in that meaning, but got to be applied to underwear; even "upper" and "lower unmentionables" appear. Today, if used at all, it refers to women's panties and bras. "Hair-do" is of U.S. origin, and began its career in 1943. In both cases, there is reason to suspect that the terms may have been devised by men, the first jocularly, the second by *coiffeurs* (hairdressers, if you prefer) for publicitarian purposes.

On the other hand, consider three additional terms showing the *-ie* suffix, "smoothie," "meanie," and "cutie." The first is traced back to 1938, and refers to a person, usually of the opposite sex, who is a clever operator. The second, derived from "mean," which is Middle English, but derived from an ancient Indo-European root that can be traced through early Germanic (modern German *gemein*) and Latin *communis*, is applied to persons by 1665, but gets to be really popular in its modern acceptance ("He's an old meanie") around 1951. The third, "cutie," arises in 1731 as a derivative of "cute," itself derived from "acute," which goes all the way back to Latin *acuo*, "to sharpen." At first it is used only in the sense of "sharp," "clever," but by 1921 it acquires a U.S. slang sense of "pretty girl." "Pie" is added on in 1948 to give us the fond appellation "cutie-pie." The first two of these three words are normally used by women, the last more frequently by men, save perhaps in the "cutie-pie" variant.

The feminine vocabulary includes a number of French borrowings, among which are names of colors that normally mean nothing to men: "beige," "mauve," "taupe," "écru." The last comes into English in 1869; its etymological meaning in the original French is "from the raw"; our dictionaries all agree that it means "unbleached," but, being written by men, they differ as to the color shade; Webster's Third defines it as grayish yellow, the Random House Dictionary as light brown. "Tulle" and "bouffant," among others, appear almost exclusively in women's magazines. A couple of other popular euphemisms like "derrière" and "enceinte" are also French, though here there is perhaps a newspaperman's touch; still, would the average man speak of a well-placed kick in the "derrière"? Would he not use other euphemisms, such as "expecting" or "expectant," possibly even "heir-conditioned," instead of "enceinte"? Of course, women have a line of fully native euphemisms, too, of which "powder room" is typical.

Next we have an entire series of extravagant adjectives to describe something or somebody that may be only mildly acceptable; they range from "wonderful," through "adorable," "heavenly," "divine," and "dreamy," to "sensational," which may have had a loan-translation assist from French *épatant*. To describe something as really funny, a woman will use "hysterical," which is altogether appropriate to her sex, since the word is derived from the Greek form for "womb." "Hysterical" begins to be used in English in 1615, in the sense of "morbidly excited," on the theory that such morbid excitement, characteristic of the feminine sex, is somehow connected with the womb. Webster's Third, in 1961, still describes "hysterical" as connected with the emotions, but the later Random House Dictionary gives the ultra-current acceptance of "extremely funny."

The use of "fun" as an adjective ("a fun party," "a fun dress," even "a fun fur," for an inexpensive fur piece that may be banged around) seems largely due to feminine influence. As a noun, "fun" goes back to 1719 in the sense of "trick," "hoax," and gets to mean "boisterous party" by 1727. Its origin is somewhat mysterious, but if, as some authorities suspect, it comes from Middle English "fon," which meant "foolish," then it was originally an adjective, and has now recovered its pristine function. Strangely, the Random House, latest of our dictionaries, does not list the adjective use of "fun." A somewhat different yet similar use (perhaps from the 1727 meaning given above) appears in Anglo-Indian, where "a fun" is used for a party at which one has fun. The expression "Have fun!"—half command, half wish—is some- times invested with sexy overtones. "Sexy" itself, which goes back only to 1928 ("sex," of course, appears much earlier) may be partly due to feminine influence.

One word that is quite current among women (it amazed me the first time I heard it, as my feminine interlocutor was applying it to herself) is "bitchy." The root word, "bitch," appears in Anglo-Saxon as *bicce* and is traced to Old Norse *bikkja*, "female dog." (I cannot help wondering whether there may not have been, somewhere along the line, an assist from Old French *biche*, "doe," from Latin *bestia*, "beast.") The first recorded appearance of "bitchy" is in 1930, with the rather uncalled-for meaning of "striking in appearance, classy." It goes on around 1940 to "sexually provocative," "having sex appeal," which seems more appropriate. The Oxford Dictionary refuses to recognize it. Webster's Third connects it with a spirit of malice or arrogance, while the Random House Dictionary defines it in two senses: "lewd," and also "malicious," "unpleasant," "selfish." There is no question that the last was the connotation in which my in- terlocutor used it, and which I misunderstood by reason of the "bitch" connotation. It seems to be superlatively a weasel word, and an excellent one to avoid.

One last feminine-inspired word, "togetherness," has been tentatively traced to Kahlil Gibran. The Oxford Dictionary refuses to recognize it, but it appears in our modern American dictionaries in the sense in which it is customarily used, to describe the full sharing of family activities, whether the various family members are sincerely interested in one an- other's doings and problems or not. Europeans, whose family life is more compartmentalized than ours, often sneer at the fact that an American candidate for public office dare not appear in public without his wife by his side, along with as many of his children as can be conveniently mobilized.

At least one popular suffix and one recent and popular prefix seem due to feminine influence, or at least designed to appeal to the fair sex, the -*ette* of "copette," "majorette," even "sanette," and the *mini-* of "miniskirt," "minicast," "minilove," and a myriad others.

A convenient transition from the feminine to the teen-age vocabulary is supplied by the teen-age magazine for youthful females, which feature such words as "deb," "sub-deb," "teen," "sub-teen," "twixt-teen," "petiteen." In the case of "deb," we have a colloquial shortening of "débutante" which comes into use in the United States in 1926 for the social élite, but to which sinister overtones are added in 1945, when it becomes popular for female gangs and female auxiliaries of male gangs to use "Debs" in their titles, as brought out by both the Random House Dictionary and Wentworth and Flexner.

"Teen" and all its derivatives stem, of course, from the numerical suffix of "thirteen," "fourteen," etc., up to "nineteen," which is straight Anglo-Saxon. There is, strangely, a coincidence in form, though not in derivation, with another "teen," also Anglo-Saxon, now archaic, which meant "harm, injury, damage, mischief"—but this is, we hope, a pure coincidence. The first use of the numerical "teen" is in the plural ("He is in his teens"), which appears in 1673. "Teenager" and all related forms do not appear until the 1930s, and Wentworth and Flexner bring out the interesting fact that American English is the only language to make special provision for this group, both linguistically and emotionally. (Other languages, of course, speak of "minors," "adolescents," "young people," "people in their growing or formative years.") They go on to point out that ours is the only country where teen-agers constitute a separate entity whose influence, fads, and fashions are handled as a thing apart. But since American influence is all-pervasive, we fear this is no longer true. France has her "Yeh-yeh" magazines and her *Salut, les copains!*" ("Hi, pals!"); and Italian teen-agers call people over twenty-five "78-revs," referring to the speed of the old short-playing records. Even Castro's Cuba has such youth groups as *Los Beats, Los Chicos Now, Los Chicos del Sí, Sí, Sí, Los Sicodélicos.*

Much has been written concerning the teen-age language, which has so many ramifications and connections that it is difficult to say where it begins and ends. In addition, it is among the fastest-changing of linguistic forms, and what is highly fashionable today may be altogether obsolete or archaic a year hence. Within my own lifetime, "hello" has been replaced by "hi," and "beat it" and "23 skiddoo" by "scram" (origin unknown; said to be possibly from the 1586 "scramble," whose origin is likewise unknown; others say it comes from German *schrammen*, "to scratch, graze, scar," itself used slangily). It comes into U.S. usage in the early 1930s, is unrecognized by the Oxford Dictionary, but given by the Random House Dictionary with a mild "informal" label, and by Webster's Third with no label at all.

Terms of approval and disapproval abound in the "turned-on" or "switched-on" generation (not even our American dictionaries list these terms). Something or somebody you like may be "way out," "something else," "in the wind" (this is more British than American), "real gone," "crazy," "the most," "the end." Note that in teen-age language "gone" is not the past participle of "go," but separates itself from its parent verb in the 1950s to assume the meaning of "great, wonderful, outstanding." "Go," on the other hand, is an exhortation to action. There is confusion between "go" and "go go"; actually, the latter is not the Anglo-Saxon verb, but French slang (*à gogo*, "aplenty," "in abundance," a discothèque phrase which presumably implies that there is lots of "action" going on). For what it may be worth, there is a Japanese *go* which is a game, a Filipino *gogo* which is a vine from whose bark soap is made, and a Gogo Bantu-speaking tribe in Tanzania. Additional terms of approval are "groovy" (or "in the groove," arising in the 1930s and referring, presumably, to the grooves of a musical record; "to groove" in the sense of "to make love" is very recent); and "grotty," used in connection with masculine long hair worn Beatle style. This word does not appear in any of our dictionaries, but one might take a stab at derivation from "grotto," which also gives us "grotesque." "Mod," long in use as an abbreviation for "modern," is defined in the Random House Dictionary as a British usage for teen-agers who strive to appear sophisticated. It has spread to American television (*The Mod Squad*).

Chief adjective of disapproval is "corny," which has gone into the universal tongue. This word first appears in 1580 as applied to beer, with the meaning "tasting of malt"; by 1825 it means "tipsy." There is another "corny" that comes from the corns on your feet, from 1707. Could the two have converged? Both have logical connotations. Some authorities link "corny" with "corn-ball," a sticky sweet; others with "corn-fed"; these, too, are logical. The word comes into use in its modern acceptance in 1935, and our modern American dictionaries define it as "true, mawkish, over-sentimental, old-fashioned."

"Square," another term of disapproval which has passed into the general language, is described as arising, in our specific acceptance, in the 1940s. Webster's Third defines it as "an outsider, one who is not in the know"; the Random House Dictionary gives "one who is not interested in current fads, a traditionalist." How the term came into being is a matter of guesswork. Wentworth and Flexner trace it to "squarehead," a term applied in the early years of this century to Scandinavian immigrants, or to "square John." Partridge claims concurrent influence from jazz musicians' steady 1-2-3-4 rhythm without variations (the band director's hand moves in the form of a square), plus the "fair" connotation of "square deal"—a person of conventional morals who tries to live right, but has little fire or imagination in his make-up.

"Upper plates" is also picturesquely applied, with justification, to the older generation.

Terms which the younger generation share with the hip-hep world of music include "cool" and "cat," "crazy," and "beatnik" (the last with its large new family, "Vietnik," "peacenik," "lunik," etc.). For "beatnik" there are three hypotheses (the suffix is the Russian -*nik* of "Sputnik," discussed elsewhere): the "beat" generation; the "beatific" advanced by Jack Kerouac, and the "beat" of music, in the sense of jazz rhythm, favored by Partridge.

"Cat" was once a tramp, or an itinerant worker. Then he turned into either a "gay cat" (inexperienced), or a "cool cat" (hep, wise, right-digging). The current use dates ·back to around 1920. Webster's Third accepts "cat" as "hot jazz devotee," but labels the expression "slang." The Random House Dictionary adds a later interpretation, "person, guy."

"Cool" implies a praiseworthy indifference to one's surroundings, a detached attitude, what conventionally might be called poise. By functional change it has become a verb ("Cool it, man!"), and a noun ("He lost his cool"). Strangely, the meanings "unexcited," "not to be excited," go all the way back to Anglo-Saxon, though the modern vogue of "cool" began in the 1950s. The Random House Dictionary further defines it as a synonym for "great," "excellent."

"Dig" is a verb that implies understanding, agreement, appreciation, particularly of certain brands of music. The word is Middle English, and seems to stem from the same source as Anglo-Saxon *dic*, which gives us "ditch." It was in U.S. slang use as far back as 1789, in the sense of "to study hard." In 1849 it turned into a noun, meaning a "diligent, plodding student." In older British usage it was used by con men in the sense of "to make inquiries, case the joint." In its modern slang sense of "understand, take notice of" ("Do you dig me?") it is found only as far back as 1941. "Zonked in" or "out of it" imply a failure to "dig."

"Bread" for money is recent, 1957, but it is encountered in the sense of "means of subsistence" ("to earn one's bread") as far back as 1719. Some teen-agers "margar" their bread, instead of "buttering" it.

The teen-age language includes some mystery words, like "fuzz" for police (no one seems to know how this use originated, though Wentworth and Flexner set its initial point in 1931), and the word variously spelled as "pazazz," "pizazz," and "p'zazz." Of interest is the fact that neither Webster's Third nor the Random House Dictionary gives any of the forms recognition, despite its widespread use. Wentworth and Flexner place its first appearance in 1951, in the sense of "power, pep," implying, but without assuming responsibility, that it may be connected with an earlier "pazazza" for "piazza." *Se non è vero è ben trovato!*

No dictionary recognizes the "pussycat" of "What's new, pussycat?" Yet "pussycat" was used of a girl as far back as 1583. There seems to be another use of the word, with application to a man ("He's a real pussycat!"), but the precise connotation in this connection remains somewhat obscure. As I have heard it used, it could mean "nice guy," but also "simpleton." The use of "bird" for a girl does not seem to have spread on this side of the Atlantic, though it has widespread use in Britain. We prefer "chick," "broad," "tomato," and at least a dozen other synonyms.

"Chick" in the expression "slick chick" (attractive girl) must not be confused with "chicken," once used the same way, but today overwhelmingly preferred in adjective use to mean "cowardly, yellow" (it is definitely an adjective: "They are chicken," not "chickens"). The word is Anglo-Saxon, but the current use dates back to 1941; again Webster's Third labels it "slang," which means it must be pretty bad. One theory is that it is an abbreviation for "chicken-hearted"; other interpretations are more scatological. Here again it is of interest to note how other languages use the equivalents of "chicken" in a figurative sense: in Italian *pollo* means a sucker; in Spanish a handsome, dashing young man.

A couple of rather sad words in this youthful language are "pad" and "pot." The first progresses, or perhaps we should say degenerates, from its sixteenth-century meaning of "straw pallet" to a "dwelling" (house or apartment), "room," "bed" ("Pad me!" is a cat's invitation to a chick to share his room and bed); then to "narcotics den" or "addict's bed." "Pot" is current slang, in use since the early 1950s, for marijuana. But what is the connection? As in the case of "fuzz" for police, no one seems to know, or even be willing to take a guess. Could there be a link with an earlier slang meaning of "slovenly, unappealing girl," or a shortened form of "rum-pot" for drunkard, or moonshine made in a pot instead of a distillery?

Along with all this and lots more, there are phrases that come into vogue by reason of initial teen-age use: "Tell it like it is!" "Sock it to me, baby!" "Do your own thing!" For the last, one wonders whether there may be a loan-translation link with Italian *cosa* of "Cosa Nostra" ("our own thing"). Once upon a time, the phrase was "Do your stuff!" "Thing" is a good old Germanic word, which in Anglo-Saxon had the meaning of "judicial assembly." Even today, the *Storthing*, or "Big Thing," is the Norwegian parliament. A *Times* correspondent recently attributed the origin of "Do your own thing" to Emerson's *Essay on Self-Reliance*; but another pointed to the fact that "thing" appears only in one (1926) edition; all others have "Do your own work."

One legitimate question: To what extent do the items of feminine and teen-age language we have presented qualify as weasel words? They are not, as a rule, meant to deceive or mystify. All they do is to proclaim that their user is a member of a certain class, and to flaunt the word-slogan like a battle-flag in the faces of mere men or of the older generation, as the case may be. "We are in the groove; you are squares!" is the implication, very squarely put (no pun intended) in the case of the Pepsi generation; very subtly, almost treacherously implied in the case of the female sex, whose giggles you almost fancy you hear as they come out with a class-word that belongs to "us girls."

Let them both have their fun. A thoroughly masculine and adult vocabulary could form the subject of a chapter, too; but then our book might be banned in Boston.

CHAPTER 6

The Plague of Journalese

Recently two unknown correspondents wrote me letters of inquiry about the precise use and meaning of words which they claimed were being bandied about in the press, "stance" and "byzantine." "Stance" was being used where "attitude" seemed indicated. As for "byzantine," which the correspondent had looked up in one or two dictionaries, the context seemed to show that "tricky" or "wily" or "treacherous" was at the back of the original user's mind, and this meaning did not appear to jibe with what was given by the dictionaries.

"Byzantine" is the more recondite and unusual of the two. The Oxford Dictionary gives it as first appearing in English in 1599, being linked with Byzantium or Constantinople, and being a term applied to music, architecture, art, and history, but with no figurative meaning that would explain the context. This time Webster's Third and the Random House Dictionary were more enlightening than the Oxford Dictionary not so much under the heading of "byzantine" as under "byzantinism," which both defined as a political and social characteristic involving the doctrine of state supremacy over the church, or, to use an equally obscure synonym, "Caesaropapism." It was only by implication that "byzantine" could be interpreted as "devious" or "tricky," but this meaning stands out clearly in other languages. Italian, for instance, even has a verb, *bizantineggiare*, "to act in Byzantine fashion," "to conceal your true thoughts," "to use double-talk," "to split hairs." This was precisely the way my correspondent

45

had found it used. To what extent can the widespread use of a word in one language justify a similar use in another?

For "stance" the situation was different. Here we have a word, in use since 1532, described by the Oxford Dictionary as originally Scottish and northern English, and used for standing-place and the posture one assumes in playing golf. The Old French *estance*, from which it comes, means the act of standing, but it branches off into a building site in other Romance languages (Spanish *estancia*, a ranch; Italian *stanza*, room or dwelling). The Oxford Dictionary does not carry it on to a figurative meaning, but our American dictionaries do ("an intellectual, mental or emotional attitude," which was the use that had irked my correspondent). This brought to my mind the very similar use of "posture," employed since 1605 in the sense of physical position or attitude, but becoming a mental or spiritual attitude by 1692, and given in that sense by the American dictionaries ("frame of mind"). Yet I had been mildly annoyed by such expressions as "tax posture" and "defense posture," which in my mind at least brought up images of someone striking a pose and then freezing in it. My correspondent had been equally annoyed, and with greater justification, by the identical use of "stance," which he probably associated with golf.

These uses are characteristic of the many language clichés that are brought into vogue by our newspaper writers and columnists. It is a well-known fact that some journalists are extremely creative, and coin words at the drop of a hat in the hope that they may be picked up and enter general usage (as a matter of fact, a good many of them do—witness Walter Winchell's "heir-conditioned," "age of chiselry," "making whoopee"). But there is another form of journalistic activity which is not so glaring, but equally penetrating—taking little-used words, some of quite ancient vintage, shining them up, and putting them back into circulation, sometimes with their traditional meaning, more often with a novel nuance.

Consider another complaint, voiced, strangely enough, by

a member of the journalistic fraternity writing in the *Christian Science Monitor*. He complains of the widespread use not only of "phased out," which might be regarded as an innovation, but of such words of long standing as "structure," "dialogue," and "single" (the last following a superlative: "the biggest single problem"). Here there is no question as to the legitimacy of the words. While the Oxford Dictionary makes no mention of "phase" as a verb, our American dictionaries give "phase out" as "to complete and then eliminate a process," such as an advertising campaign. "Structure," even as a verb, is given as "rare" by the Oxford Dictionary, but has grown tremendously in America, as attested by Webster's Third and the Random House Dictionary. "Dialogue," as a conversation involving two or more participants, goes back to 1597; only the 1966 Random House Dictionary defines it as an exchange of opinions designed to lead to an amicable settlement of controversies, which is the sense objected to. The use of "single" after a superlative does not seem to bother anybody except the *Monitor* writer. What he really had on his mind, I suspect, was the frequency with which these words appear in journalese. They are vogue words, linguistic fads, and the journalists are responsible for their spreading out far and wide.

A list of words of fairly long standing which the newspapers have plucked out of semi-retirement and plunged into active modern life could be quite extensive. "Cavalier," whose history is traced elsewhere in this book, seems to be such a word ("He gave me cavalier treatment," in its present-day usage). There is "cohort," a word that first appears in English in 1489 in its quite classical meaning of one-tenth of a Roman legion; by 1719 it expands its meaning to cover any company or band; the subtle, modern innovation, which we have reason to attribute to the columnists, is its application to individuals in a group, or even singly ("a gangster chief accompanied by one of his cohorts"). There is the "gap" of "credibility gap" and "generation gap," which starts out in Old Norse, gets into early English in the sense of "breach" or "mountain pass," and by 1523 acquires the less physical meaning of "hiatus"; then, perhaps because of Lost and Beat Generations, it becomes the "generally wide difference in attitudes" of Webster's Third or the "wide divergence or disparity" of the Random House Dictionary, and the number of gaps multiplies.

"Viable" is a word that comes to us from French in 1825. When I first saw it I was in doubt whether it came from French *vie*, "life," or from Latin *via*, "way, road." It would have made sense either way, since a "viable state of affairs" would be not only one you could live with but also one you could pass through. The dictionary definition says "capable of existence or being, workable." It is much overused.

"Ploy" is given by the Oxford Dictionary as a Scottish and northern English word for trick, escapade, game, hobby, first discovered in 1722. The Random House Dictionary says it is Middle English and derived from French *ployer*, and suggests that its original use is military, as indicated by its derivative "deploy" and its use in antiquated military terminology for "maneuver," while Webster's Third thinks it is a back-formation from "employ." Its modern newspaper use is as "stratagem," and Roscoe Drummond used it five separate times in a single one of his daily columns—definitely one of those vogue words that fascinate writers, even though no one really knows where they come from or what they mean.

"Explosion" is a fairly old word (1656, with figurative use from 1817, "a bursting forth in sudden fashion"). In recent times everything has become an "explosion." Bruce Bliven is credited with having started the "population explosion" in 1899, but there is also a "freedom explosion" which was properly publicized in connection with the new African nations. Crossing linguistic and national boundaries, we find Italian newspaper men speaking of *esplosione dialet-*

tale, illustrated by such writers as Carlo Emilio Gadda, who features over-numerous dialect forms in his otherwise impeccable Italian writings. The Random House Dictionary defines "explosion" in this sense as "sudden, rapid, big increase."

Many words and expressions that start elsewhere, on stage or screen or in army barracks, travel on newspaper wings until they become firmly established in the language. This seems to have been the case with forms like "gadget," "gimmick" and "gremlin," "bikini," "young marrieds," and "The Greats," "The Bomb," "The Pill," "Beautiful People," "jet set," and "socialite," the subtle semantic shift of "hopefully," semi-slang forms like "tribalize," "stateside," "know-how," "whodunit," "whydunit."

"Gadget" first appears in 1886 in nautical parlance, with the meaning of "small tool"; by 1915 it gets to mean "accessory"; by 1925 it acquires the slang meaning which permits it to enter Wentworth and Flexner. But Webster's Third cites several specific legitimate uses, and the Random House Dictionary defines it as "mechanical contrivance." The origin is, of course, unknown, though Partridge tentatively advances "gage," measuring instrument, reduced in French to a diminutive form, *gaget*.

"Gimmick," definitely U.S. slang, and therefore unreported in British works, save by Partridge, first appears in 1928. The Random House Dictionary links it with both magicians' tricks and electronic devices, and Webster's Third defines it as "new, ingenious device," first used in connection with dishonest gambling. In Partridge's view, it has a complicated derivation from a combination of "gimbal" (itself from "gemel," twin, coupled), "gimcrack," and "trick." If it is true that it was in origin applied to a dishonest gambling device, one might also consider the possibility of "gimme" (colloquial for "give me") with an *-ik* suffix borrowed from Yiddish or Russian.

For "gremlin" there is more assured derivation from Royal Air Force slang, in 1941. The gremlin is viewed as a mysterious elf-like being that exerts a baneful, disruptive influence on planes, and Webster's Third suggests a combination of "goblin" with Irish *gruaimin,* "elves." The real point with all these highly colloquial forms is that they are publicized and spread by the press, which fastens upon any picturesque innovation from whatever quarter.

Or take the case of "bikini." This is the name of an island of the Marshall group where a big U.S. atomic test took place in 1946. Some imaginative newsman, probably French, thought of comparing the devastation wrought at Bikini with the devastating effect upon males of the new style feminine bathing costume (another French newsman even coined "monokini," for a topless bikini). Today, Bikini Island and its atomic test are quite forgotten (who ever thinks of Eniwetok, another island where a similar atomic explosion took place?); but the beach bikini is still very much in pictorial evidence as well as in the news.

"Young marrieds" and "the Greats" of something or other are two expressions that have always grated on my ear, though that is neither here nor there. They represent the process of free, unbridled functional change for which English is renowned. "Married," as a past participle, ought not to be given a plural form. Only our most permissive dictionary, Webster's Third, recognizes and exemplifies this expression, which nevertheless appears in all newspapers in the land. "Great" got to be applied to persons as far back as 1649, but received no plural *-s* even when it had a plural meaning. The British, however, beat us to that phenomenon, applying the expression "the Greats" to the final comprehensive college examination for the A.B. degree in 1853. Otherwise, down to 1945 we find "the Great" exclusively used as a plural form. Lait and Mortimer are credited with applying "the Greats" to various fields of human endeavor in 1948, and today both Webster's Third and the Random House Dictionary give us "great" as a noun with a choice of plurals, with or without the -*s* marker. Newspaper use of "the Greats" is not only general, but extremely widespread ("the Greats of music," "of literature," "of baseball," etc.).

There is nothing about either "bomb" or "pill" that is unconventional save their use, preferably in capitalized form, to refer to a specific yet generic "Bomb," of the atomic or hydrogen variety, that is destined to obliterate life on earth, and to a specific "Pill," used for contraceptive purposes. Both uses are sensational and highly journalistic. Interestingly, "the Pill" was used around 1957 with reference to the Hiroshima atom bomb. "The Loop," a contraceptive device widely used to replace "The Pill," now appears in the form of artistic earrings, which some women delicately wear. Whether this is a covert invitation to "safe" sexual relations is unknown to this writer.

"Jet set" pertains to the social columns. It is a recent creation, as evidenced by its non-appearance in the Oxford Dictionary or even Webster's Third. But the 1966 Random House Dictionary defines it as an ultrafashionable social group that spends its leisure time traveling by jet plane from one international resort to another. There is little information as to when and where "socialite" came into being, though a popular magazine claims it first appeared in its pages. It does not appear in the Oxford Dictionary, and is rather briefly defined in the American dictionaries as one who is prominent in social circles.

"Hopefully" is given only by the Random House Dictionary in its newly acquired sense of "it is hoped" ("Hopefully, we shall get there on time"). It has been suggested that perhaps the English word was influenced by German *hoffentlich*, used in the "it is hoped" sense at a much earlier date.

Among semi-slang forms, "tribalize" is attributed to Marshall McLuhan, but reported in none of our dictionaries.

The base form "tribe" goes back to Middle English, "tribal" to 1632, "tribalism" to 1886. Come to think of it, there is no good reason why we shouldn't have it if we feel we need a word to express the concept of "to handle something in tribal fashion."

"Stateside" is described as a military coinage, and said to have made its first bow in the overseas military newspaper *Yank* in 1944. Webster's Third defines it as "pertaining to the continental U.S.," and goes on to speak of a "Statesider in Guam," while the Random House Dictionary defines it as "in or toward the U.S." One wonders about the precise function of -*side* in this expression, favored by the news media.

"Know-how" is old U.S. slang, and the Oxford Dictionary traces it back to 1857. It no longer causes eyebrows to rise. Neither does "whodunit," which is traced back to 1930, but which some attribute to Wodehouse, others to Donald Gordon. Analogy being what it is, a book reviewer used it to coin "whydunit," where stress is on the motive rather than on the butler. The Random House Dictionary calls "whodunit" informal, Webster's Third waxes stern and calls the parent phrase "Who dun it?" substandard.

There is a use of "complex" to apply to any group of buildings that drew fire from a columnist. The noun use of "complex" to describe a complex or composite whole goes back to 1652, and our American dictionaries allow it in the sense of "group of related units," which would seem to cover the building situation.

The use of "contact" as a verb, arising in America in 1929, was roundly criticized at first. Opposition has now subsided, but there is another, adjectival use of "contact" in "contact sports" which appears on sporting pages and may be criticized at any moment. Only Webster's Third defines this usage as a sport involving violent bodily contact, such as football. "Decisioning," used in some government circles, has at times been criticized on the ground that Middle English "decide" is, after all, the verb, and "decision," appearing in 1490, should be the noun. Webster's Third offers "to decision," but only in the sense of "to win a decision over," not as a synonym of "to decide." "Standing" is a favorite news word, which has found favor even on the other side of the ocean; French has borrowed it as *le standing*.

Newspaper coinages which may have only the value of nonce-words frequently appear. One such is "at-onceness," recorded by none of our dictionaries, yet somehow pleasing to the ear and the sense of linguistic need. Another, forming part of an ever-growing family described elsewhere, is "sex-ploitation." "Crunch" has recently appeared as a noun in the sense of "showdown," "moment of truth."

Lastly, there are language clichés, oft-repeated phrases, to which tired newspaper writers are prone. Some, like "Time is running out," are fairly traditional. Others, like "in the know," have slangy overtones.

To what extent is all the material listed above weasely? Only to a mild degree. The news writer is often forced to take the line of least resistance, and defer to his readers. If he can employ a vogue word to make his meaning clear, why should he bother seeking linguistic variety and multiplicity? Repetition serves his purpose. Also, he shares with other classes of intellectuals the desire to impress his fellow-man, if not with the profundity of his knowledge, at least with his easy and complete familiarity with that segment of the vocabulary that everybody is currently using. In going along with a fad, he often not only spreads it, but comes close to initiating it. But if the advertising man uses words to sell products, the politician to sell ideas, the labor leader to sell hours and wages, should the newsman not be allowed to use words to boost circulation?

CHAPTER 7

Progressive and Retrogressive Education

"Educanto" is the name coined by Mortimer Smith, editor of the *Bulletin of the Council for Basic Education*, for the "mumbo jumbo developed by educators to confound the public in general and inquisitive parents in particular." His article gives numerous samples of this jargon. Particularly fashionable among users of Educanto in 1968, it seems, are "relevant" and "relevancy," referring to an education that concerns itself with objects of immediate interest, such as pot and riots, as opposed to ancient events and personalities, like the American Revolution and Shakespeare.

Among the more technical terms are "paraprofessional," to refer to a mother who helps the kindergarten teacher to put on the children's overshoes; "resource center" (or "instructional materials resource center"), a library with audio-visual aids; "media coordinator," someone who operates a tape recorder. "Pupil stations" for "desks" appears elsewhere. In addition, there is some truly specialized gibberish: a "curriculum" may be described as any of the following: "life-oriented," "learner-centered," "merged," "multi-media," "multi-mode," "empirically validated."

Another educational expert with a cool perspective, Fred M. Hechinger, writing in *The New York Times Magazine*, had previously joined forces with Dr. James B. Conant in an all-out attack on Pedageese, a language that has among its distinguishing marks a strong reluctance to call things by their proper names (a slum, for instance, becomes in Pedageese an "older, more overcrowded area," possibly by reason of the condescending implication of "going slumming"). The weasely aspects of Pedageese, says Dr. Hechinger, are designed (1) to create the impression of great professional wisdom; (2) to make the uninitiate believe that essentially simple or even non-existent problems are terribly involved and require very expert effort; (3) to do for education what Madison Avenue does for commercial products; (4) to make things appear better than they are. One might remark that in this classification, headings 1 and 2 connect Educanto with both scholarly and political gobbledygook, while 3 and 4 stress the publicitarian side and link up with the wonder world of advertising.

Your true educationist, says Hechinger, will never use the verbs "talk" or "speak" while "communicate" or, better yet, "verbalize" are available. School children don't learn reading, writing, and speaking; they learn the "communications arts" or the "language arts." (In these phrases "arts" may be replaced by "skills.") The "manipulative skills" (but not "manipulative arts") are those things they learn to do with their hands. If they are acquiring a foreign language mainly by listening and repeating, it is an "aural-oral" method that is being employed. Then there are "evaluations" of "felt and unfelt needs" (the first means letting the child have his way, the second doing what the teacher wants done); "vital learning experiences" (such as raising the hand if you want to leave the room); "corrective feedback" (telling the pupil what he did that was wrong); "controlled" and "pioneering experiments," leading to "new and unique courses" which are as often as not "breakthroughs." "Motivational research" creates an "intensive focus" which leads to the discovery of a pupil's "untapped potential" or "latent ability."

The terminology of an earlier day included the "educational process" (or "experience"); the "effectuating" of a "constructive approach"; "education for the whole child" (apparently it is also possible to educate half a child); the

universal "challenge"; the now largely discredited "I.Q.";
"education for leadership" (it apparently did not occur to
the educators that there should also be some measure of
"education for followership," or we would have all generals
and no privates). The earlier "education for life adjustment"
(or "for social living," or even "for expanding democracy")
got at one point to be replaced by "education for the air
age," quickly followed by the "space age." Other traditional
terms included "enrichment," "cultural immersion," and "re-
orientation." (One critic ironically suggested putting into
operation a Reorient Express that would get us there faster.)
Fully technical terms were "certification" (basically, a union
card entitling you to teach in the elementary and high schools,
as the Ph.D. entitles you to teach in the colleges); "workshop" (not in the literal sense, but as a sort of seminar course
in the problems and practice of teaching); and the ubiquitous
"methods of teaching" (any subject; in my own language
field, I have often wondered whether there is enough difference in the methods, as apart from the content, of teaching
French, Spanish, and Italian to warrant separate offerings).
Another favorite term of twenty or thirty years ago was
"integration," used in the sense of making the various parts
of a curriculum dovetail so as to bring out the basic unity
of human knowledge; but then "integration" came to be applied in a racial sense, with fully and partly "integrated"
schools, and the old meaning fell into desuetude.

"Desegregation," a synonym for the newer use of "integration," was very much in vogue for a while. Then came the
new tendency to "decentralization," which meant pretty
much a return, under new management, to the "separate but
equal facilities" of old. The result is that now we are faced
with two opposite processes carried on at once, but usually
in different localities.

The vocabulary of juvenile delinquency blends education
with violence, as well as with psychology. The "problem

child" (some impatient columnist once equated this term with "pain in the neck") is generally "insecure," "frustrated," "repressed," "confused," "maladjusted," "emotionally disturbed" (or "emotionally unstable"). Some, but by no means all, of the problem children are "underprivileged," "socially disadvantaged," or "culturally deprived." They display unusual "behavior patterns," and often turn, later on, into "dropouts." It may or may not occur to the educationists that their troubles may in part stem from the "permissive" type of education that began with John Dewey and continues with Dr. Benjamin Spock. Two typical symptoms of the existence of problem children are "parent resentment" (the parents blame the teachers for what goes on) and "teacher bias" (the teacher, being human, occasionally loses patience and takes it out on the pupil who is giving him trouble and disrupting his class).

H. I. Phillips, a columnist of an older day, writing in the *New York Sun*, once defined "insecurity" in the educational sense as a child's feeling that he can't knock out all the school windows and beat up the teacher; "frustration" as a deep conviction on a child's part that his freedoms are violated if he is not allowed to set fires in the classroom and thumb his nose at both teachers and rules; "repression" as a condition that arises when mother asks the children to get home from the high school dance within forty-eight hours of its conclusion; "confusion" as difficulty in making a distinction between right and wrong; "maladjustment" as having been so treated by tolerant parents that at the age of fourteen the child cannot reconcile himself to a command, rebuke, or suggestion; and "underprivilege" as the state of not getting twenty-five dollars a week spending money and not being permitted to stay out all night.

In a more serious vein, it may be worth while to look at some of these word usages historically. A cross-section of words appearing in this chapter (some, like "underprivileged," are discussed elsewhere in the book by reason of their even more widespread use in other fields) shows that a few ("aural-oral," "whole child," "cultural immersion") appear in none of our major dictionaries. This may in part be due to their being word groups of which the individual parts appear (both "whole" and "child," for instance, go back to Anglo-Saxon), in part to the fact that they are truly items of a professional jargon.

Others illustrate surprising semantic and chronological developments. The Oxford Dictionary gives "drop out" only as a verb, while the modern American connotation of the noun "dropout" appears in both our American dictionaries. "Workshop," which the Oxford Dictionary traces back to 1562, but lists only in the sense of "place where manual work is done," is given by both American dictionaries as a seminar for the free exchange of ideas and demonstration of methods, often conducted in the summer, for and by adults. "Potential" is listed by the Oxford Dictionary as an adjective dating back to Middle English, and used as a noun only since 1817, but the only British uses of the noun by 1932 were in the fields of grammar (the potential mood) and physics; Webster's Third, while not very specific, applies the word to people, and the Random House Dictionary very specifically speaks of a "talent or ability not yet developed." The Oxford Dictionary gives us "break through" as a verb, but "breakthrough" as a noun only in a military sense (1924), and spells it with a hyphen; both Webster's Third and the Random House Dictionary give the latter in its modern acceptance as a "significant, often sudden advance in scientific knowledge." The Oxford Dictionary does not recognize "I.Q.," but dates the fuller "intelligence quotient," followed by "test," in 1921 ("quotient," in the field of mathematics, goes back to Middle English); both Webster's Third and the Random House Dictionary are fully up-to-date in its educational use. The Oxford Dictionary does not list "maladjusted," though "maladjustment" (1833) appears; the American dictionaries define "maladjusted" as "lacking harmony with one's environment," and Webster's Third even exemplifies with "maladjusted child." "Insecure" is traced back by the Oxford to 1649; Webster's Third and the Random House Dictionary, particularly the latter, apply it specifically to persons. "Permissive," from late Middle English, according to the Oxford Dictionary, is not directly linked with education by either of our American dictionaries, though Random House comes close when it exemplifies with "a permissive family." "Frustrated" is carried back by the Oxford Dictionary to 1500 in the sense of "baffled"; Webster's Third defines a frustrated person as one filled with a chronic sense of insecurity, and the Random House Dictionary also applies it to persons, though not in its educational sense. "Verbalize" appears in the Oxford Dictionary as used from 1609 in the sense of "to use many words," but only from 1875 in the sense of "to express in words"; both American dictionaries stress the latter meaning. "Disadvantage" is given by the Oxford Dictionary as a transitive verb meaning "to cause disadvantage to someone"; Webster's Third and the Random House Dictionary list "disadvantaged" separately as an adjective, with the meaning of "lacking the resources or conditions necessary to achieve an equal position in society," and Random House even exemplifies with "disadvantaged children."

A curious reversal appears in the case of "certification." Here the Oxford Dictionary traces the word back to 1440, and gives as a "modern" definition the "certification of elementary teachers." This highly specialized educational use is given by neither Webster's Third nor the Random House Dictionary.

The euphemistic "language arts" does not appear in the Oxford Dictionary, though both component parts go back to Middle English. Both our American dictionaries list the combination in its American pedagogical acceptance; neither one, however, cares to accept the alternative "communications arts," though "communications" is defined as including language. The ambivalent "integration," which the Oxford Dictionary traces back to 1620 but lists in neither of its current American acceptances, educational and racial, is fully defined in both senses by our American dictionaries, though Webster's Third emphasizes the educational use (to organize teaching matter in such a way as to unify or link the subjects), while the Random House Dictionary prefers a more psychological interpretation.

Among the more recent educational creations and uses, two deserve special mention. One is "under-achiever" for a student who won't work, along with "over-achiever" (an even thornier problem to the educators), the student who insists on doing all his work, and a little more besides. Here the root word, "achieve," goes back to 1607, coming from French *achever*, which in turn goes back to Latin *ad caput* (*venire*), "to come to a head." In its present-day acceptance, "to bring to a successful conclusion" seems the best definition.

"Exciting" is a word that stems from Latin *excito, ex-cio*, "to call forth." As far back as Middle English, "to excite" means "to rouse up," while from 1850 on it acquires the added meaning of "to move to strong emotion or passion." In its present-day dictionary connotations, "exciting" means "absorbingly interesting," "arousing excitement" (in turn defined as "augmented or abnormal activity"). In educational parlance, "exciting" is being used more and more as a synonym for "mildly interesting." A writer for a children's encyclopedia, for instance, is asked to make the chapter on language "exciting" to the youthful readers. Literally, this would mean making them jump up and down and shout with joy merely because they have discovered that English and German are related. Here is a glaring case where the force of a word has been sucked out of it, weasel fashion, to a point where its original meaning is impaired. This puts the modern "exciting" in the same class with "darling," "doll," "heavenly," and "divine" as handled by certain feminine users. Incidentally, there is also a political use of the new version of "exciting." Mayor Lindsay wants to make New York City a more "exciting" place to live in. Perhaps a few more police, fire, and ambulance sirens will do the trick of "arousing augmented or abnormal activity" in the psyches of residents and visitors alike.

This cursory survey seems to lead to certain conclusions: the educational community, like all specialized fields, has developed its own professional terminology, which is legitimate. The use of parts of this terminology to dazzle and befuddle the layman has definite weasely features. Reactions to this practice have been fully exemplified, both by totally lay members of the community, like Phillips, and by fraternity members, like Hechinger and Smith.

As in most weasel-word fields, it is hopeless to seek a remedy. All we can do is to describe and exemplify the practice, and warn the reader to be on his guard the next time he finds himself in contact with educational experts or is caught up in a discussion of school budgets.

Historically, it is of interest to note how large a part of this jargon has come into existence since the appearance of the Oxford Dictionary in 1932. But this situation is duplicated in the majority of fields.

CHAPTER 8

Scholars and Scullers

The widest street in New York is said to be 120th, because it separates Columbia University from Teachers College. The separation is symbolical.

South of the street are the scholars; to the north are the educators, or educationists, or pedagogues. The chasm between them is broader than the Wide Missouri and deeper than the Grand Canyon.

For reasons best known to themselves, American educators and scholars have placed the dividing line between their respective specialties at the end of high school and the beginning of college. The reason may be economic. A high school education at the expense of the taxpayers is the recognized right of every American youngster. College, in the old days, had somewhat stricter rules of admission; but in addition it was generally in private hands, and only the rich or moderately well-to-do could afford it. It mattered little that the course of study was merely a continuation of what had begun in high school, with identical and often repetitive subject matter. It mattered little that the real line of demarcation lay between the undergraduate college and the graduate school, where the true work of scholarship began. It mattered little that in most civilized countries of the world this situation was recognized, with the university, corresponding to our graduate school, set apart from the elementary and secondary school system. The American educational world had a very simple way of getting around this. A one-horse undergraduate college would give itself the proud title of "university," justifying it by putting in a couple of "graduate" courses in a couple of specialties. In the larger and more legitimate establishments, integration of college and university was achieved by requiring professors who were primarily research scholars to add undergraduate courses to their offerings, whether or not their tastes ran that way. The line of demarcation between high school and college accordingly deepened.

Today the high school teacher is primarily interested in methods, the college professor in content and, at least theoretically, in higher research. It matters little that what is required for most undergraduate courses is a good teacher, not a researcher. The research requirement for all college teachers is embodied in the Ph.D. prerequisite, and in the now famous slogan "Publish or Perish" (not recognized in any of our major dictionaries; it means that an undergraduate college professor, even if he holds a higher degree, must continue to publish "scholarly" writings to hold his job or qualify for advancement, regardless of his merits as a classroom teacher).

Under the circumstances, there has grown up an entire vocabulary of scholarship, which is as far apart from that of pedagogy as is Columbia University from Teachers College. Along with this vocabulary of scholarship there is a jargon that flourishes among the "scullers," those unfortunate teachers who find themselves compelled to pose as scholars in order to gain their livelihood. Samples of this are "union card" for the Ph.D. degree; "slave market" for the annual conventions to which college and university professors repair to read learned "papers" to one another and thereby prove their scholarship, and where heads of departments interview and hire promising job applicants. There are such terms as "egghead" for "intellectual," which in turn has been defined as "trained thinker," although often the training is more in evidence than the thinking. The term "egghead," non-apparent in the Oxford Dictionary, is defined by Webster's Third as one with intellectual interests or pretensions, and listed by the Random House Dictionary as an informal synonym for "intellectual," with overtones of baldness due to excessive study. There is the very recently coined "uncollege route," describing the process, so common in an earlier day, whereby an individual gifted along manual, mechanical, or business lines achieved success in life without bothering to go through four years of a so-called "liberal" education.

The use of "liberal" in connection with "education" or "arts" is itself a splendid example of weasel wording. The Oxford Dictionary defines the "liberal arts" as those worthy of a free man; opposed to "servile" or "mechanic"; the implication seems to be that a gentleman goes to college, while a member of the slave or lower class learns a trade, and lets it go at that. This particular use of "liberal" goes back to Middle English, but few of those who speak today of a "liberal arts" college remember this interpretation. It nevertheless accounts for a great deal of the snobbishness in the matter of "going to college" that pervades all segments of American society.

The legitimate vocabulary of scholarship is extensive. It exudes in all its parts a faint aura of stuffiness and pomposity, which to some extent places it in the weasel class.

There is, to begin with, the word "scholar" itself, with its derivatives "scholarly" and "scholarship." While the origin of the word lies in the Greek *schole*, "leisure" (again we have the concept that only free men had leisure to devote to study and discussion, while the slaves toiled and performed the menial and mechanical tasks), it gets into Middle English, where at the outset it seems to have been synonymous with "schoolboy" (French *écolier*, Italian *scolaro*, still carry that meaning almost exclusively, and should not be used to translate English "scholar"). But late Middle English brings in the sense of "erudite" or "university student." The meaning of "student receiving a stipend or emolument to enable him to pursue his studies," as in "Rhodes Scholar," begins in 1511; "disciple of a famous teacher" in 1577. "Scholarship," first appearing in 1535, eventually branches off to mean both the "stipend that a scholar receives" (interesting is the use of "Fulbright," unadorned, since 1946, to denote a government scholarship for study abroad under the Fulbright Act) and the "attitudes, methods, and traditions of the erudite world," which is what concerns us here. "Ivory tower," first conceived by the French literary critic Sainte-Beuve and applied by him to A. de Vigny, is one of the more imaginative creations of the scholarly mind, though highly descriptive of scholarly practice.

"Academic" is often used as a substitute for "scholarly." It stems from Academe, the name of a public grove in Athens where Plato taught, itself derived from a semi-mythical character, Academus, of whose estate the grove is said to have once formed a part. The word is often used in combination, as in "academic freedom," which in one interpretation refers to the right to teach and study without fear of political or other interference, in another to the right arrogated by some professors and students to conduct themselves any way they please, academically, sexually, and in connection with narcotics, riots, and forcible seizure of buildings. It is perhaps significant that the combination, explained at considerable length by our American dictionaries, which trace it back to German *akademische Freiheit*, does not appear in the 1932 Oxford Dictionary, though it must have been already in existence at that time.

"Survey" and "study" are much used words, but they are shared with many other fields. More specific are "paper" (in the scholarly sense, it refers to a minor contribution read at a gathering or convention; when preceded by "term," the paper becomes the forerunner of more serious diseases, such as the "thesis" and the "dissertation." (The former more often leads to the "M.A.," or *Magister Artium*, degree, the latter to the Doctor of Philosophy; but the two terms are to some extent interchangeable.) "Research" is an all-purpose word. Research features "reports," "consultations," "sources" (in connection with the last, it has been said that if you copy from a single source it's plagiarism, but if you copy from multiple sources it's research). "Literary influences" are relentlessly tracked down. Often what results from years of research is not a single scrap of new information or original thought, but a mere compilation of what everyone else has said or thought on the subject; in this case, the fruit of the research is described as an *état présent*, or summary of the present stage of our knowledge on the topic. (This term is so foreign that none of our major dictionaries report it, even as a foreign expression; nor does it appear in our specialized glossaries of foreign terms and expressions.) Almost as often, however, we have an "analysis in depth," which was once described to me by a colleague in the literary field as going into every minute of the waking and even the sleeping hours of the subject of the research in an effort to find out what had made him tick. This once led a man who is one of the few truly great scholars in the literary field to remark that the trouble with Dante was that he had not been a Dante scholar, and consequently had not thought of supplying the answers to the questions that twentieth-century scholars would ask about him.

Among administrative terms in the field are "seminar" and "pro-seminar." The former appears in the Oxford Dictionary as an importation from German in 1889; the latter appears in the Oxford Dictionary only in the form "pro-seminary" (1774), a preparatory school for a seminary. But whereas the seminary is an institution, often for the training of the clergy, the seminar is a group of graduate students, each working on his own individual problem, but meeting at stated times under the guidance of a professor. Webster's Third is the only one of our dictionaries to define the pro-seminar as a group affair conducted like a seminar, but open to advanced undergraduate students. "Multiversity," said to have been coined by Dr. Kerr of Berkeley, is defined in the Random House Dictionary as a "large, decentralized university with many separate campuses." Other recent coinages are the "minicourse" and "maxicourse" suggested by Dr. Warren Susman of Rutgers University in connection with his far-reaching plan of academic reform.

We also have the "residence units," now replacing the older system of points, which at least told the graduate student where he stood in relation to his total course requirements; and the "ad hoc committee," an august body of scholars from various fields selected by the administration for a specific purpose, which is often to pass on the qualifications of a man in a totally different field who is up for appointment or promotion. The literal meaning of *ad hoc* is "for this."

The fields of scholarship (and scullership) are many and varied. Of the three great divisions (the Humanities, the Social Sciences, the Physical Sciences), the last is best reserved for a special chapter. In the first two fields there is much common ground, since both deal primarily with "Man" (spelled with a capital) and his multiform manifestations. It is here that we find the "Great Books" (Webster's Third alone defines these as those classics which are basic to Western culture; some, by the way, are truly great) and the "Great Tradition." (Occasionally other "Greats" are added, such as the "Great Issues," but these are by their very nature passing phases.) Here abound such adjectives as "pragmatic," "transcendental," "immanent," "evolving," "sophisticated" (now so often borrowed by the military, who use it in connection with weapons of destruction); such nouns as "awareness," "perspective," "ideology" (Allan Porter claims that this is a translation of German *Weltanschauung*, which is rather a "world perspective" or "outlook on the universe"; the dictionaries, however, trace it back to French *idéologie*, coming into English in 1796; the term originally meant "the science of ideas," but it has been distorted to mean a particular set of ideas peculiar to a person or, more often, a group); "sociology" (here again Porter claims that this was a late nineteenth-century American creation, borrowed by the Germans, who took a fancy to it, as *amerikanische Wissenschaft*; but again the dictionaries trace it back to 1843 and label it a borrowing from French); "self-realization," "continuum," "senescence," "cosmos," "determinism"; such verbs as "to redefine," "to restructure," "to confront," "to mythologize"; such word combinations as "frontier of freedom," "ecumenical move-ment," "new level of dimension," "patterns of regulation and control," "evolutionary transcendence," "form of process," "democratic world community," "education as power," "max-imum creativity," "ever-restless quest," "dawning age of space," "galactocentric universe," "unitary man," "Man on Earth," "homo progressivus," "wholenatured organic will," "newer foresights," "socio-cultural dimensions," "widely af-firmative trends," "cross-," or "inter-," or "pan-disciplinary venture."

To try to define or translate into everyday terms many of these words and expressions would be a hopeless task; not because they have no meaning, but because they have mean-ing only in the concept and context of the person who is using them at a given time.

There is little question that any and all of these terms have legitimate uses in highly restricted situations. The trouble with them is that they are all too often bandied about not so much for purposes of clarification as for ends of obfuscation—what French writers have happily summarized in the twin expressions *jeter la poudre aux yeux* and *épater le bourgeois* ("to throw dust into people's eyes" and "to bedazzle the lay-man"). It is mainly in this connection, which unfortunately makes too frequent appearances, that they may be described as weasel words.

A fair sample of the language of scholarship in action can be had from a report conceived and written by a dean (who shall be nameless) of a highly reputable institution of higher learning which shall also be nameless. It will be observed that the use of academic gobbledygook is occasionally fraught with lamentable lapses in syntax and spelling which we can only hope may be indicative of carelessness rather than of ignorance:

"The provincialism of education for the professors evolved as a result of increasing complexities of practice and equally from the false pride of self-importance. . . . The very productivity of all professions have [*sic*] caused social changes that rebound to new demands on the professions and society. . . . When confronted with this new responsibility we have often withdrawn to the synthetic parish limits we have established as the boundaries of our activity or blundered into the breech [*sic*] with simplistic panaceas, simplistic because they arise out of ignorance. . . . Via this procedure we have only achieved a rounded man with an extremely short radius. . . . The interrelationships exist—the synergisms are explosive. . . . No longer can we tolerate schisms in educational objectives. Integration at all outputs is necessary to solve real problems. . . ."

Unfair as it may seem to cite the above sample sentences out of the full context, it is nevertheless our experience that the full context fails to clarify them. We can see vague, undefined striving toward a goal. But what is the goal?

This is to a large extent the basic trouble with the world of scholarship.

CHAPTER 9

Science and Pseudo-Science

Science Is a Sacred Cow was the title of a book that made the best-seller list some years ago. The author was at pains to point out that the attitude of a good many scientists was that science could do or say no wrong. "Scientific" is a magic word in the modern world, and there is even a fairly recent coinage, "scientism," which does not appear in the Oxford Dictionary, but is defined by our American dictionaries as the assumptions, methods, techniques, practices, points of view, etc., characteristic of scientists, and which the Random House Dictionary further describes as being foisted by some scientific-minded scientists upon other fields, such as social studies and the humanities; a third interpretation is "scientific and pseudo-scientific language," and this puts it squarely in the weasel class.

Another sacred cow in the field of science is "laboratory," differently stressed by Britain and America, and cut down to "lab" for short; as long as something is sanctified by the laboratory and its experimental practices, it must be regarded as holy and proved.

Perhaps more than in any other field, however, there is a legitimacy to the peculiar vocabulary of science in all its branches. Things have to be called by names that will be significant to all the practitioners in the field, even if they are meaningless to the uninitiate. It is estimated that of the million or so words in modern English (or any modern civilized tongue, for that matter), fully half pertain to science and technology in all their ramifications.

To the extent that a science departs from purely physical aspects and links up with the study of man and his doings, there is a tendency for the vocabulary to take on "scientistic" or weasely features, and be used for effect. It is therefore natural that we should seek our subject matter rather in those sciences which have human angles (anthropology, linguistics, psychology) than in those that deal with inert matter and principles (physics, chemistry, biology, mathematics). At the same time, some words used in the field of science in general or in some very physical sciences in particular strike us not only by reason of their imagery, but also because they tend to get into the common everyday language with meanings that are often distorted.

On the other hand, there are a few rare words that sound weasely but aren't. "Artifact" (something man-made, or worked on by human beings) sounds like a very recent coinage, but the Oxford Dictionary informs us that it has been around since 1834. It sounds as though it had been constructed to bear out a thesis, but none is discernible. So use "artifact" without fear or hesitation, along with "ventifact" (1940), defined by the Oxford Dictionary as a stone shaped by the wind. "Quasar" (a heavenly body that emits strong radio signals, but is at a tremendous distance from our galaxy) is so recent that only the Random House Dictionary reports it. It sounds like one of our astronomical terms borrowed from Arabic, but it is simply a telescoping of "quasi-stellar." "Pulsar" has very recently been coined to describe a star that emits regularly spaced radio signals. "Thrust," "impact," "response," even "breakthrough," are common to too many fields to draw particular attention when used, or even overused, in scientific talk. Then there is meteorology's "degree-day," not in the Oxford Dictionary, though the first element goes back to Middle English and the second to Anglo-Saxon. Our American dictionaries both give it in its current newscast acceptance: the number of degrees below a norm (usually 65° Fahrenheit) that occurs in the average temperature on any given day. If the average temperature of January 1st is 34 degrees, then January 1st is a 31-degree day. What confuses the layman is the hyphen, which should precede, not follow "degree" to give the correct impression.

"Decibel," originally an electrical term, is now popularly used as a unit of loudness in acoustics. "Feedback," not in the 1932 Oxford Dictionary, but defined in both American dictionaries as the return of part of a computer's output to the input, has now become generalized beyond all reason.

Then there are those two very current expressions, "atomic fission" and "chain reaction." In the first, the "atomic" part goes back to 1678. But despite its popularity, no dictionary recognizes the combination (the Random House Dictionary does offer "nuclear fission," which is far more precise), probably because of its contradictory meaning, "splitting the unsplittable ("atom" is from Greek *a*, "not" and *temno*, "cut," "split," while "fission" is from Latin *findo*, "to split"). "Chain reaction" has penetrated the general language to the point that in Webster's Third the generalized meaning of "chain of linked events, one provoking the next" gets precedence over the specialized chemical and nuclear meanings. It appears in the Oxford's addenda only as a nucleonic and chemical term. "Domino theory" is a good replacement, particularly in international affairs.

Two choice terms from the computer field are "computerize" and "binit" (or "bit"). With respect to the former, the Oxford Dictionary is so far behind that it not only ignores the verbal form (so does Webster's Third, for that matter), but gives "computer" only in its human sense, "one who computes." Our ultra-modern Random House Dictionary gives "computerize" as "to calculate or automate by computer," and the "computer" itself has in accordance with modern standards become an electronic machine. Objection, if any, is to the verbal derivative. "Binit" and "bit" are both telescoped forms of "binary digit" (1 or 0, in computer talk and the New Mathematics). "Bit" is particularly confusing, not only because it is a telescoping of a telescoping, but because it gets mixed up with the traditional "bit" that comes down from Anglo-Saxon.

A true language invariably develops a slang. The language of science is no exception. Here is a word like "garbage," which has a very definite meaning to the housewife and the sanitation department. But it is used in two different scientific divisions with two additional and somewhat slangy meanings. In Computerese, it refers to irrelevant information produced or included in the computer's output. In space talk, it means miscellaneous objects in orbit, usually material ejected from or broken away from a space vehicle or satellite. Webster's Third ignores both uses; the Random House Dictionary recognizes only the second. In its generally accepted sense of "refuse," this word goes back to Middle English, which seems to have taken it from Anglo-French. The Oxford Dictionary says it is especially used in the United States.

"Glitch," the malfunction of a rocket, is, like earlier "gadget" and "gremlin," a pure coinage and is still unrecognized by any dictionary. "Debug" means to locate, correct, and remove errors in a computer program. "Eyeballs in" and "eyeballs out," not given in any dictionary, describes the astronaut's experience of acceleration and deceleration at the lift-off and the firing of retrorockets, respectively. "Housekeeping," which in its ordinary acceptance goes back to 1538, is used in Computerese to denote the programmer's setting up of storage and buffer areas prior to the execution of a program.

A prefix like *mega-*, taken from the Greek word for "big," is slangily used by scientists in such forms as "megabuck" ("one million dollars"; this form is recognized only by the Random House Dictionary), coined on the analogy of "megavolt," "megacycle," etc., where the meaning of "one million" has been somewhat arbitrarily assigned. "Megamistake" is a similar humorous coinage, but goes back to the original Greek meaning of "big." *Nano-* is similarly used to denote one-billionth ("nano-second," one-billionth of a second), but does not seem to have given rise to any humorous coinages. A *New York Times* writer coined "Uniquack" for an imaginary computer, on the analogy of the existing Univac. "Mobot" has recently appeared for "motor robot."

The vocabulary of anthropology offers some interesting uses, of which perhaps the most significant is "culture." Anthropologists, ever in the forefront of equalitarian movements, have regaled us with a meaning for the word which is almost directly at variance with the older acceptance. Derived from Latin *colo*, "to till, cultivate," "culture" has been in use since 1510 in the sense of "the act of development by education, discipline, training; enlightenment and refinement of taste acquired by intellectual and esthetic training; the particular stage of advancement of a civilization." Since 1805, the Oxford Dictionary reports, it has meant "the intellectual side of a civilization." Our older Webster's gives as synonyms "enlightenment, civilization, refinement." It remained for the anthropological scientists, linguistic and otherwise, to give it the new twist that appears in the 1961 Webster's Third: "The total pattern of human behavior and its products, depending on man's capacity for learning and transmitting; the distinct complex of tradition of a racial or social group." As applied by the anthropologists, it is quite legitimate to speak not merely of ancient Greek or modern French culture, but also of the Stone Age "culture" of a cannibal group in the interior of New Guinea. If burying one's aged parents alive, or cutting up, pickling, and eating one's enemies, Congo or Angola style, is a local custom, it becomes by definition part of the "culture" of the group that carries on these practices. This deliberate debasement of the word "culture" means that we can no longer use it as synonymous with civilization, enlightenment, or refinement, under penalty of being laughed at. Perhaps we should resurrect the German *Kultur* from the days of Kaiser Wilhelm to supply us with a suitable differentiation for what too often amounts to two opposite meanings of the same word.

"Folkways" and "mores" are words that do not draw quite the same fire. The former does not appear in the 1932 Oxford Dictionary, though both portions are Anglo-Saxon in origin. Our American dictionaries define the word as the social habits or way of life of a group. "Mores" was apparently not in use in 1932, to judge from the Oxford Dictionary, though we cannot conceive of anyone brought up in the English public school tradition not recognizing Cicero's "O tempora! O mores!" Webster defines it, roughly, as the "culture" of a group, the Random House Dictionary as the group's "folkways" of central importance. This would seem to make both words acceptable substitutes for the anthropological use of "culture."

A professional linguist may perhaps be forgiven for poking a little fun at his own specialty in the matter of its use of words, particularly those that have spilled over into the field of education and language-learning. There is, for example, the coinage of "linguistician" (on the analogy of "mortician," perhaps?) by a member of the linguistic fraternity, who was disturbed by the fact that "linguist" lent itself to too much confusion with "polyglot" (the latter being defined as a person who can handle many languages, but not necessarily the techniques of the trade, while the "true linguist," in extreme cases, could be a person who speaks no language except his own, but is competent in the techniques and, above all, the terminology). "Linguistician," of course, does not appear in the Oxford Dictionary (it was coined, if memory serves, in the 1940s), but "linguist" has been in use since 1588 in the sense of "one who knows many languages," and only since 1817 in the sense of "philologist." Webster's Third and the

Random House Dictionary both define "linguistician" as a student, expert, or specialist in linguistics. Random House further has the good grace to label it "rare."

All sorts of picturesque terms grew up around the new language-learning methodology based on the spoken rather than the written word: "aural-oral," "audio-lingual," "mem-mim" (this is a telescoping of "memorization" and "mimicry"), even "talkie-talkie." These terms are regarded as so specialized that none of our dictionaries reports them, though "audio-visual" appears in the 1966 Random House Dictionary.

Two interesting terms are "internalization" and "overlearning," for the practice of memorizing words and expressions in the foreign language to the point where they are automatically used as reflexes. The former does not appear in the Oxford Dictionary (though "internal" goes back to 1509), but our more recent American works both give it in the sense of "incorporating through learning." Somehow the word, and even the definition, jar. They are reminiscent of heart or bone implants, or of the Chinese practice of swallowing the written prescription along with the medicament prescribed. The second term, not in the Oxford Dictionary or the Random House Dictionary, though both parts go back to Anglo-Saxon, appears in Webster's Third, as "to continue study even after one has attained a criterion level of performance." The question rather spontaneously arises "Why waste your time?" At any rate, both terms are symbolical of the Pavlov dog methodology advocated by some modern "linguisticians" or "linguistic scientists" who believe in conditioned reflexes rather than the working of the conscious mind.

Three terms highly revered by the American school of linguistics are "value judgment," "judgment-free," and "usage." The last has indeed gotten into usage. The first two, though based on Middle English and Anglo-Saxon forms, are far from popular. The Random House Dictionary alone defines "value judgment" as a subjective estimation of the worth of something. The second expression means that your "scientific" opinion is free of the subjective judgment value. A sample of a value judgment would be an inference on your part that language forms like "dem guys" and "us-'uns" are intrinsically inferior to "those men" and "we" because they do not conform to educated standards. It would be taken as a super-value judgment for you to decide that you do not care to employ as a copy-reader the man who habitually uses them. Here a social and political *Weltanschauung* gets mixed up with linguistics, and the results may be summarized in "Leave your language alone!" because "One man's language is as good as the next."

"Usage" is subtler. The Oxford Dictionary informs us that the word goes back to Middle English for what concerns behavior, to 1697 for what concerns language. The Webster's Third and Random House Dictionary definition that is pertinent is "the customary use of language." "Whose customary use of language?" is the question that naturally arises. The doctrine of usage has been raised into a cult by some linguistic scientists, who believe in settling problems of usage by nose-counting. If enough people say "Who did you see?" instead of "Whom did you see?" or "I laid on the couch for an hour," that is Usage, and the tradition-conscious minority had better conform or get its tongue chopped off. Again, the socio-political implications range far beyond the field of language, linguistics, or even linguistic science.

The language of psychology long antedates that of psycho-analysis, introduced by Sigmund Freud at the beginning of the present century. Kant's "categorical imperative," the concept of a moral obligation that is universally binding, or what man had long known as the "command of conscience," may certainly be defined as a psychological even more than a philosophical term. "Paranoia" goes back to 1857, though some of its specific attributes (compensatory megalomania, persecution and grandeur delusions, etc.) were gradually added. "Phobias" and "manias" were in vogue throughout the second half of the nineteenth century. Even "schizophrenia," which Webster's Third defines as a separation between the intellect and the emotions, and the Random House Dictionary as delusional behavior (both avoid the popular "split personality" definition) antedates the Freudian concepts.

The Oxford Dictionary, which sets the first appearance of "psychoanalysis" in 1910, defines it as the analysis of the unconscious mind through free association. The Random House Dictionary even more specifically describes it as the relationship between the conscious and the unconscious, and Webster's Third brings in the technique of the analysis of dreams. The adjective "Freudian," which also first appears in 1910, has to do with psychoanalysis and dreams according to the Random House Dictionary, but Webster's Third adds a new acceptance developed through popular usage, that of "sexy" or "smutty." Here, perhaps, is where the scientific ends and the weasely begins.

Basic to the Freudian concept are such widely used weasel terms as "ego," "superego," "id," "libido." The Oxford Dictionary records "ego" (1824) and "id" (1893), but defines the first only in its old philosophical acceptance of "the thinking subject," and the second as a term used in biology. Webster's Third warns us that "ego" has had numerous definitions since the days of Descartes, all antedating the Freudian use. In its Freudian acceptance, the "ego" is that part of the individual which reacts to the outside world, mediating between the "id" and the individual's social and physical environment (one could equate it with the ancient "reason"). The "superego" (1923) appears in Webster's Third as a mostly unconscious development of the ego through a process of instruction, ruling the ego and keeping it on the straight and narrow path; the Random House Dictionary places the superego in a mediating position between ego drives and social ideals, and equates it to the old-fashioned conscience. The "id" (1924; a Latin translation of an original German *es*) appears in Webster's Third as the source of energy for both the ego and the libido, and in the Random House Dictionary as a set of unconscious impulses. The "libido" (1913) is energy derived from biological urges and instinctual desires. A more specialized writer, Adam Margoshes, presents the ego as that part of the personality that deals with reality, and that the individual feels is his true self; the superego as conscience; the id as sexual and aggressive instincts and the source of the unconscious; and the libido as sexuality, the basic psychic energy. "Reason," "conscience," "instinct," and "lust" would seem to be the traditional equivalents of the four Freudian terms, and could rather easily be used to replace them.

Additional terms from the vocabulary of psychology are "inferiority complex," which Webster's Third informs us is a loan-translation from German, and defines as a sense of inferiority leading to timidity on the one hand (the Random House Dictionary prefers "reticence"), to over-aggressiveness on the other; the various psychological family relationships with overtones of incest (the "Oedipus complex," a libidinal feeling toward one's mother, with the viewing of one's father as a rival; the "father image" or "father figure," which is in a sense the feminine counterpart of the Oedipus complex, with an idealization of one's father, but with the added feature of a projection or transfer of this idealized image to another male person; the "sibling rivalry," a feeling of competition between brothers and sisters, with occasional sexual overtones). Then there are the three types or characters defined as "Oral," the sucking and biting type representative of the first stage of individual development, which in later life assumes aspects of passive dependency coupled with occasional aggressiveness; the "Anal," or second stage, deriving pleasure from bodily functions and manifesting itself by excessive neatness, miserliness, self-discipline, and obstinacy; and the "Genital," representing the third stage of full sexuality, normality, independence, and decisiveness.

An attempt was made some decades ago to carry the individual's experiences back beyond his infancy, while still in his mother's womb. This was labeled "Dianetics," but was rejected by the majority of psychologists. Webster's Third calls it an "extra-scientific system," the Random House Dictionary a "non-scientific theory." Here the "engram" (1914), a memory trace, or protoplasmic change in the nervous system as the result of a prenatal experience, may cause somatic troubles that may be cured through appropriate psychotherapy.

Two terms that have spilled over into the field of medicine are "psychosomatic" and "somatopsychic." The first implies that a physical disease may have mental causes, the second that a physical disease may cause mental troubles. There is a tendency to overuse both terms when no other explanation is available for what is ailing the patient.

Other terms that have spilled over into the field of sociology and human relations include "alienation," "isolation," "adjustment," "self-actualization," "self-fulfillment," and "self-realization." "Alienation" has been recognized since 1482 in the sense of "mental derangement," is exclusively used in that sense by many languages, and may still be so used in English; the new concept that has been introduced in recent times is that of "estrangement of affections." "Isolation," used since 1833 in the sense of separation from persons or solitariness, has more recently acquired two additional connotations: social withdrawal, and the divesting of emotional content from an idea or memory; the first is highly popular, the second quite specialized. "Adjustment" goes back to 1644, but not in the psychological sense, described by our more recent American dictionaries as a psychological process leading the individual to adjust to society and accept conformity of behavior; its most important derivative in this sense is "maladjusted," which has spilled over into the educational field. Of the three "self-" concepts, only "self-realization" is recognized by the Oxford Dictionary, which traces it back to 1876, and defines it as the fulfillment by one's own efforts of the possibilities of self-development. This idea is accepted by both Webster's Third and the Random House Dictionary, though in somewhat different terms. (Webster's Third stresses the fact that it is best for man to fulfill himself if he has the gifts, while the Random House Dictionary emphasizes getting what you desire through your own efforts and fulfilling your potential capacities.) "Self-actualization," incidentally, is rejected by both American dictionaries, though it appears in specialized works. "Introvert" and "extrovert" have been in English since the seventeenth century, but in psychological use only since 1916 and 1918.

Two interesting slang forms appear in psychological parlance. One is "momism," a recently coined expression not recognized by the Oxford Dictionary, which Webster's Third defines as excessive adoration of one's mother, with Oedipal overtones, while the Random House Dictionary stresses domination by a mother image, corresponding to the "father figure." The other is "hung up," in the hippie sense of fixated, a term so recent that it is not recognized in that acceptance by any of our major dictionaries; the nearest Webster's Third and the Random House Dictionary come to it is "delayed" or "detained," which in a sense define the word as it is used in the East Village.

"Psychedelic" is a typical Youth Explosion term, so recent that only the 1966 Random House Dictionary carries it. It is applied to something (like a drug) that brings "pleasure, calm, perception, even creativity." The derivation given is Greek *psyche*, "soul, spirit," and *deleo*, "to make visible or evident"; the idea being that a psychedelic drug brings your soul out into the open; but the thought occurred to me as I checked the Greek roots that the -*delic* part could just as legitimately stem from *deleomai*, "to destroy," and that if this derivation is preferred we get a meaning that seems closer to reality, "that which destroys the soul, mind, or spirit." Who is responsible for these things? The hippies, yippies, and flower children, or the older generation, with its Cult of

Youth and contempt of the experience that comes (sometimes, at any rate) with age? But we are not all guilty, nor need we all abdicate.

To what extent do the words we have listed qualify as weasel words? They are legitimate enough in specialized parlance. It is only when they are allowed to spill over into the general language, and to aid and abet in creating states of mind among the laity that they become objects of suspicion. When "Freudian language" can be equated with "sexy or smutty talk"; when "inferiority complex" and "adjustment," or the lack thereof, are used as a justification for anti-social conduct; when "libido," "id," "Oedipus complex," "father image" come into play to account for certain forms of sexual behavior, there is reason for the word-conscious layman to be on his guard.

CHAPTER 10

The Sanctity of the Law

There is a widespread belief to the effect that gobbledygook is a phenomenon of modern civilization. Nothing could be further from the truth. Centuries before gobbledygook became the tool of modern bureaucrats, it was a majestic manifestation of the medieval legal mind. To prove this, all you have to do is glance at an ordinary present-day legal document (a will, or a contract, for example) whose wording reflects not the language, or even the slang, of today, but the quaint turns of phrase employed by men of the law in the days of William the Conqueror, or even of the Romans of Cicero's day. Half of our specifically legal terminology is Latin: *mandamus* and *certiorari*, *per se* and *pro forma*, *habeas corpus* and *nolo contendere*, *affidavit* and *prima facie*; not to mention terms that have spilled over into the language of politics, like *pro tempore* (often abbreviated to *pro tem*) and *sine die*, horribly mispronounced to the point where the first part sounds like the trigonometric function and the second like the synonym for "perish"; others that have become popular to the point of entering gangster and western slang (*alias*, *alibi*, *posse*), or are used in trade (*bona fide*), or are erroneously welded together (*subpoena*, which started out as *sub poena;* cf. *sub rosa*, *sub judice*, etc.), or are the products of the worst kind of hybridization (*veniremen*, half Latin, half Anglo-Saxon). Mispronunciations aside, do the modern lawmen who use them know something about their origin? *Affidavit*, which the Oxford Dictionary traces back to 1622, not only refers to a written and sworn statement, but literally means "he swore." The *posse* of the westerns, traced back to 1583, is the infinitive "to be able," used with the force of a noun, "power," and when accompanied by *comitatus*, which was added on in 1626, means "the power of a following." The ugly *veniremen*, in use since 1444, in its Latin part goes back to *venire facias*, "you may cause or order to come," and refers to the summoning of a jury.

For that part of legal terminology that goes back to the French of the Normans and their Middle English-speaking descendants, we have such terms as "escheat," from Old French *escheoir* (modern French *échoir*), which normally refers to the lapsing of a given time period, but specifically means the reverting of fiefs or possessions to the crown or state by reason of non-performance of conditions imposed for their enjoyment; "escrow" (1598) from French *escroue*, a roll or scrap of paper, entrusted by two parties to an agreement to a third party to be delivered to one of them, but only after the fulfilling of certain conditions; "mayhem," basically the same word as "maim," going back to 1472, is derived from Old French *mahaigner*, itself derived from a Germanic root, and means to do bodily harm in such a fashion as to partly incapacitate the victim on a permanent basis; "change of venue," of Middle English origin, where the French *venue* is the "place of coming" of the jury, in modern legal parlance means removal to another county, usually because it is impossible or difficult to collect an impartial jury in the locality where the crime has occurred. The "grand" and "petty" juries are also of French origin ("petty" is French *petit*, "small," and "jury" is from *jurer*, "to swear"). Also French are those twin forms which are not synonymous, but represent two different offenses: "assault and battery," in use since 1447, where "assault" represents the threat to do bodily harm, and "battery," from *battre*, "to beat," the bodily harm itself; or "libel and slander," both Middle English, where the first represents character defamation in writing or pictures, coming from an originally Latin *libellus*, "little book," while "slander," from French *esclandre* (which also gives us "scandal") is defamation by speech or gesture. Another double sample, this time from Greek, is "digamy" and "bigamy," of which the first betokens remarriage after divorce or the death of a spouse, and is legal, the other the state of being married to two different persons at the same time.

It is difficult to attach the charge of weaselry to the above expressions and make it stick, though they often confuse the layman. They are all specific and denote definite concepts, without which our body of laws could hardly function.

More confusing, perhaps, are other legal word-combinations such as "adverse possession" (this means occupation of premises by one who is not the legal owner, with no acknowledgment of or permission from said owner; in other words, the state of being a squatter; Webster's Third reminds us that after twenty years of adverse possession the squatter often acquires a legal claim to the property); "constructive eviction," which is serious interference with the use of a rented space, such as erecting a wall in front of windows to shut off light and air from the unwanted tenant; "tenancy by entirety," which means that a husband and wife own a property jointly, and if one dies everything becomes the property of the other.

Weasely aspects are in evidence when we come to certain legal formulas, such as "sum in hand paid" and "party of the first part." But while these may be confusing to the layman, there is in evidence no purpose to confuse. With "due process," however, we come into a more doubtful area. Webster's Third defines this as a course of proceedings in accordance with the law, while the Random House Dictionary has it as a limitation in a federal or state constitution, restraining the actions of the government within bounds of fairness. What are the bounds of fairness?

"Due process" is said, among other things, to justify the principle, often enunciated, that it is better that a hundred guilty persons escape punishment than that one innocent person should suffer unjustly for a crime he did not commit. Granted that no one wants innocent people to suffer, one may nevertheless entertain doubts regarding the hundred guilty who escape punishment; not so much because society fails to exact its measure of retribution, as because those guilty men are turned back on society to commit more crimes and visit suffering upon an additional hundred innocent victims. Do a known criminal's potential victims have no rights, human, civil, or otherwise? A court that frees a self-confessed murderer on a technicality would seem to bear responsibility for any harm that criminal may do in the future.

"Supreme Court decision" is another term subject to weasel interpretations. Were such decisions as sacred as some believe, they would also be immutable. This is emphatically not the case. More times than we care to admit, the Supreme Court has reversed itself in its interpretation of the Constitution. Were it not so, we would still be honoring the Dred Scott Decision and the Fugitive Slave Law, or, at the very least, the "separate but equal facilities" principle. This emphatically does not mean that Supreme Court decisions should not be observed, but simply that they should not be regarded as unchangeable. The very term "constitutionality" can lend itself to weasely abuses, since what is constitutional in one period may not be constitutional in another.

The "Fifth Amendment" has lent itself to glaring abuses, the "Fourteenth" to serious divergences of opinion, but no part of the Constitution has been more widely misinterpreted, by justices and laymen alike, than the First Amendment, paraphrased into the principle of "Separation of Church and State." All that the Amendment itself says is that there shall be no established religion in the United states, paralleling such institutions as the Church of England, whose titular head is England's temporal ruler. This hardly justifies the banning of non-denominational prayer from the schools, or the refusal to allow children who attend denominational schools to enjoy the benefits of transportation, books, and school lunches which are paid for by all the taxpayers, including the parents of the children attending the denominational schools. "Separation of Church and State" is here used as a mask for the rankest kind of atheistic arrogance on the one hand, of religious bigotry on the other.

One slogan that achieved a certain effect in recent times was the labeling of a certain Supreme Court decision "One man one vote." The decision dealt with a very far-reaching change in the structure of state legislatures, for which no parallel was suggested or hinted at in connection with the federal government, where each state, large or small, and regardless of its population, is still entitled to two senators. There may or may not be merit to the decision itself, which might very logically lead our state legislatures in the direction of a unicameral structure. But the slogan "One man one vote" had the merit of sounding extremely democratic and equalitarian, and formed an effective sugar-coating for the Supreme Court pill. Two other phrases used in connection with Supreme Court decisions that acquired the status of slogans were Franklin D. Roosevelt's "nine old men," and the "with all deliberate speed" of the school desegregation issue.

Among all legal expressions that lend themselves to weasely interpretations, there is one that deserves nomination for the Weasel Award. "Juvenile (or Child) Offender" is a jewel of understatement created by welfare workers and a judiciary subject to political pressures. Suffice it to say that while a child (to which a "juvenile" is equated) is described as a human being "somewhere between birth and puberty" (which is legally set, in British usage, at fourteen for males and twelve for females), the 1961 Webster's Third informs us that the Juvenile Court, to which the Children's Court is equated, takes care of "offenders" up to the age of eighteen, while a "juvenile delinquent" (or "offender") is defined in some states as going up to sixteen, in others to eighteen, in others to twenty-one. The laws invariably prescribe all sorts of cushions for these "juvenile" or "child" offenders, who as often as not do not have their misdeeds entered on their police records and are remanded in the custody of those same parents who could not train them properly in the first place. All this may have been socially beneficial in the days when boys of sixteen and seventeen broke a window accidentally while playing baseball in the street. Today they rob, rape, and kill. Putting these activities in the same category with a ten-year-old playing hooky from school is, to say the least, unrealistic. But here we are not concerned with legal or sociological aspects, but only with semantic ones, such as the connotation aroused in the mind of a newspaper reader who finds out that a hulking sixteen-year-old accused of a rape murder by stomping his victim to death has been remanded to Children's Court, and his name is withheld lest he should have a blot on his record in later life.

After this array of words and expressions that confuse the issues and befuddle the layman, there is one expression, "the Rule of Law," which deserves mention, particularly in its definition given by Supreme Court Justice Abe Fortas, in reply to those who invoke "civil disobedience" and "nonviolent" refusal to comply with a law as a justification for such criminal acts as physical attacks upon policemen and firemen, robbing stores, occupying university buildings by force, rioting, looting, and burning: "Both the law and the individual must accept the result of procedures by which the courts, and ultimately the Supreme Court, decide that the law has or has not been violated, that it is or is not constitutional, and that the defendant has or has not been properly convicted."

This "Rule of Law" is basic to the survival of our civilization.

CHAPTER 11

The Politics of Happiness and the Happiness of Politics

Bureaucratic gobbledygook is by its very nature weasely, since its guiding principle is never to say in one short word what can be said in ten long ones. Its motivation is said to lie in the fact that bureaucrats are often either scholars or lawmen, and therefore naturally inclined to the practice of obfuscation; but to an even greater degree, it seems to be due to the unspoken desire to evade, or at least spread, responsibility for decisions, and to "pass the buck." (In this connection, President Truman's motto "The buck stops here" is significant.)

Among typical gobbledygook creations are such expressions as "36 calendar months" for "three years," "in short supply" for "scarce," "implement" (verb) for "use"; such verbal derivatives as "finalize" (1942) and "definitize." (Only the first appears in the 1950 Addenda to the Oxford Dictionary, but both are in evidence in our more recent American dictionaries; the Random House Dictionary translates the first into "put into final form," while Webster's Third offers as synonyms the shorter "finish," "complete," "close," and lists an Eisenhower quote as an example.) There are coinages like "disincentive" (1951) and "dissaver" (1946), which are not in the Oxford Dictionary or, surprisingly, in the Random House Dictionary; but Webster's Third gives and exemplifies the first, and defines the second as one who shows an excess of consumption over savings; "negative saver" has been occasionally used as a synonym. "Guideline" and "indicator" appear, but only Webster's Third shows for the first the transition from a rope that helps you over a difficult crossing to a directive or suggestion issued by government to business and labor, so that both may consistently ignore it. The second term is quite old and generic, but none of our dictionaries records it in the governmental sense of a statistical bellwether registering the health of the economy. One of the most picturesque coinages in this division, "senior citizen," defined by the Random House Dictionary as a person over sixty-five, usually retired on a pension or social security, is so recent that it does not appear in the 1961 Webster's Third. It has drawn much fire from critics who condemn it as a rank euphemism, and one of them suggested that we label babies "junior citizens" or "junior Americans."

The language of politics has recently had a comprehensive dictionary written about it by William Safire, and his long and precise word-histories make it unnecessary to go into such expressions as "mugwump," "stalwart," "gerrymander," "lame duck," "log-rolling," "carpetbagger," "pork barrel," "filibuster," "grass roots," "mending fences," "machine politics," "landslide," "smoke-filled rooms," "smear," "whispering campaign," "slush fund," "middle-of-the-road," "itch to run," or even Johnson's very recent "nervous Nellies" for people who were apprehensive about the Vietnam war. He overlooks, however, Henry Wallace's "more abundant life" for what Roosevelt was trying to bring into being during the Great Depression, but to which former President Herbert Hoover added the codicil "without bacon," referring to the mass slaughter of little pigs designed to bring up the price of pork. There is also the use of "corner" in the phrase "prosperity is just around the corner," used by the same President Hoover at the depth of the depression, and curiously repeated in a somewhat different context by Secretary of State Dean Rusk with reference to the war in Vietnam ("The war in Vietnam is turning an important corner," uttered on March 9, 1963). "Giveaway" is another barbed term, which Safire describes at length in its earlier acceptance (concessions of natural resources made by the government to private interests), but which is also applied by irate tax-payers to the government's foreign aid program. Both uses seem to be derived from "giveaway programs" on radio and television.

In the more immediate past, and particularly in the 1968 nominating and election campaigns, there was undue stress on public opinion polls designed to indicate how the voters' preferences ran. Since such polls were based on a very small cross-section of the population, and since they showed wide fluctuations from poll to poll and from week to week, a newspaper coined the expression "to Gallup into the lead." Faith in the accuracy of the polls, periodically shaken in the past (the *Literary Digest* poll in the Roosevelt-Landon race in 1936; all polls in the Truman-Dewey race of 1948) was further shattered by the inconsistencies of the Gallup and Harris polls in the matter of Nixon vs. Rockefeller as the Republican convention approached, as well as the wrong conclusion pointed to by the final Harris poll just before the election.

True weasel usages are indicated by a certain number of political expressions of more or less recent vintage.

There is, to begin with, the American use of "politician" in a disparaging sense, where British usage has it merely as "one who is engaged in politics." Almost any American politician would feel offended and hurt at being described as a "politician." Safire reminds us that George Washington, no less, initiated the American practice when in his Farewell Address he referred to "the mere politicians," and speculates that the rebellious American colonists may have been riled at an earlier date by the lack of sympathy for their grievances displayed by British "politicians."

"Favorite son" is a presidential candidate who has no hope of being nominated, but tries to hold his state's delegates together at a convention, for bargaining purposes. He is sometimes left holding the bag, as happened to Ohio's Governor Rhodes and New Jersey's Senator Case at the 1968 Republican convention. "Freedom's Favorite Son," applied to George Washington in the late 1780s, is Safire's choice as the origin of the expression.

"Parity" is a price for farm products meant to give the farmer equal profits with those of a pre-established base period; the government then guarantees to purchase, at 75 to 90 per cent of "parity," any of the covered farm commodities that the producer has not succeeded in disposing of to his own satisfaction. But in return, the producer must pledge not to plant the covered item beyond a certain stipulated acreage. "Parity" and "price support" lend themselves to sloganeering in predominantly agricultural areas.

"Pay as you go" is a favorite slogan of governors affected by tax-and-spendomania, who offer, as the sole alternative to a hike in taxes so that you may "pay as you go," a bond issue, with costs deferred till a later time, but with interest to be paid on the bonds. There is, as a rule, a third alternative, known as "tightening the belt and cutting out the pork," but it is unpopular with "tax, spend, and elect" politicians, who are inordinately fond of four additional weasel words: "patronage," "plum," "lulu," and "pump priming." The first, in its political sense of bestowing jobs and benefits upon the deserving, goes back to 1769. The second is an appointive job which is also a sinecure; it comes from the expression "shaking the plum tree," originally circulated by Matthew Quay, a Pennsylvania political boss, in 1885. The third was coined out of "in lieu of," and refers to fixed payments made to New York State legislators and government appointees "in lieu of expenses"; it is said to have originated with Al Smith, and combines the acoustic features of "lieu" with the slang connotation of "lulu," an expression of enthusiastic admiration traced back to 1886 ("She's a lulu!"). The last, based on the well-known principle of pouring a little water down an old-fashioned farm pump to saturate the sucker so that it will start bringing up water, was coined during the early depression years of Roosevelt's administration, and means pouring federal funds into the economy to get it started again.

"States' Rights" is an ancient doctrine, based on the constitutional separation of powers between the federal government and the states and people (see the Tenth Amendment in the Bill of Rights). It can be overdone, and also underdone. It was the philosophical cause of the Civil War even more than the slavery issue, and looms large even today, as proved by Governor George Wallace of Alabama.

"Elder statesman" has been traced back to 1929, when it was applied to Elihu Root. It should mean a statesman who has retired from active duty, but still exercises advisory functions. Its greatest beneficiary, however, was Bernard Baruch, a Wall Street speculator who became the trusted advisor of FDR, but never held public office, elective or appointive. Like "senior citizen," the term lends itself to purposes of biting sarcasm.

Among more recent political creations, "hooverize" goes back to 1917, having at first been applied to Herbert Hoover's food regulations during World War I, and to his later program of food aid to stricken Europe; but at the outset of the Great Depression the term got to be disparagingly used to signify what Hoover, as President, was doing (or not doing) to end the slump and unemployment.

"Happy days are here again!" was the title of FDR's campaign song in 1932. It is occasionally resurrected by the Democrats in extenuation of their more recent failures. "Nothing to fear but fear itself" was coined by Roosevelt in 1933, but there is some question that he may have plagiarized it from an earlier, similar but not identical phrase coined by Thoreau; it makes a splendid, weasely slogan.

"Common Man" was the coinage of Henry Wallace in 1942. No one ever bothered to define this "Common Man," whose century this was supposed to be; but the term sounded good, and appeared even in loan-translation form. (Guglielmo Giannini, an Italian demagogue who enjoyed brief vogue after the fall of Mussolini, used *L'Uomo Qualunque* as the name of his short-lived party.) The "Forgotten Man," much used by Roosevelt, was coined in 1883 by a Yale sociologist, William Sumner.

"Do-nothing Congress" (the 80th) was a phrase coined by Harry Truman in his campaign against Dewey in 1948, and was among the slogans that won him the title of "Give-'em-hell Harry." Actually, all the 80th Congress had done was to turn down some of Truman's more advanced "social" legislation proposals. "Think tank" was used by Truman in the sense of "brain," but had been previously coined in 1946 in the sense of "brain trust," or more precisely, a group of scientists and scholars employed by private industry and the universities, but whose research talents would be at the government's disposal when and if needed.

"Irish Mafia" was a 1961 coinage (origin unknown) used to describe the group of Bostonians of Irish descent who flanked John F. Kennedy when he came to power. "Mafia" is the name of a secret Sicilian organization, going back to the Middle Ages, which took part in the struggles to free the island from French rule; later it turned into a semi-criminal society, distinguished by opposition to the established government and a penchant for visiting vengeance and sudden death upon its enemies; still later it degenerated into a racket, American gangster style. Both the earlier "Black Hand" and the current "Cosa Nostra" are said to be American offshoots of the Mafia, but there is no definite proof of the fact. The word itself is of obscure origin; some claim it comes from Arabic *mahyah*, "boasting," others from Old French *mafler*, "to swallow up." Its use in English dates back to 1875.

"Tax-sharing," coined by Walter Heller in 1964, is a plan to use federal tax revenues in excess of federal needs (an extremely unlikely contingency) to be turned over to the states to use as they see fit. This plan overlooks the fact that the federal government already makes vast contributions to states and municipalities in the form of grants-in-aid (over which, however, Washington exercises a decisive measure of control). The expression fits in on the one hand with Barry Gold-water's "brokerage fee" (the federal government taxes the inhabitants of the states, then returns to the states part of the take minus a brokerage fee); on the other, with Mayor John Lindsay's "Urbanaid" and Nassau County Executive Eugene Nickerson's "Localaid" (see p. 97).

Coming down to the recent past, we have a new use of "new," which is one of the oldest and most Anglo-Saxon words in the language. This ancient adjective is now applied, *à tort et à travers*, to individuals ("the New Nixon," "the New Humphrey"), movements ("the New Left," "the New Politics"), even to things that antedate recorded history ("the New Violence"). Of course, "new" is one of the all-time favorites of the advertising agencies ("It's NEW!"). But why its current extension to persons, movements, and manifesta-tions? Is this a part of the Cult of Youth, the Cult of Change? There was once a feeling of comfort that people drew from the opposite of "new" ("Old Hickory," "Old Siwash," "the Old Homestead," "the Old Folks"). What has happened to it? Is this a symbol of our civilization on wheels, in which nothing is allowed to age, mature, or mellow? Or is it ap-plied in irony and derision?

In the case of political figures, notably Nixon, the use of "new" may have been designed to counteract another expres-sion current among the former Vice-President's opponents, "loser syndrome." "Syndrome" (a running together), bor-rowed from medical parlance, has the original English mean-ing (1541) of "concurrence of symptoms pointing to an identifiable disease"; by later extension, any concurrence of phenomena that point one way. Its application to Nixon presents very debatable features. Nixon won his way into various political offices, including those of Representative and Senator. His two-time victory with Eisenhower may in part be attributed to the popularity of his running mate, but there are too many voters who are fully aware that in case of death or disability of the President, the Vice-President serves out the balance of the term. Nixon's defeat by Kennedy in 1960 was of the hairbreadth variety (something like 100,000 popular votes out of nearly 70 million), and presented some doubtful features which might still lend themselves to investigation. His only clear-cut defeat came when he ran for Governor of California against Pat Brown. This hardly constitutes a "loser syndrome," as abundantly proved by the 1968 election.

Another interesting term in this field, though it is legitimately used, is "consensus," which appears in English rather late (1854) and means "general agreement," "agreement in opinion" (Latin *consentio*, from which it springs, literally means "to feel with"). Its implications are not as strong as those of "unanimity," favored by totalitarian regimes, but rather indicative of a majority so large as to be practically overwhelming, even while leaving room for a small token opposition. (Lyndon Johnson once suggested something like one Senator out of a hundred.) Consensus may be achieved by propaganda, by friendly persuasion, by boondoggling, perhaps by a little arm-twisting. Federal grants help it along. So does the Attorney General's office. So do tax reductions which have to be countermanded almost as soon as they are granted. Consensus, however, becomes more and more difficult to achieve as time goes by, and the realities of economics and foreign affairs come to the fore.

Slogans are of signal help in achieving a consensus, but their beneficial effect, like that of aspirin, is temporary. Proof of this lies in the fact that the slogan has to be changed every few years. We have passed from "New Deal" to "Fair Deal" to "New Frontier" and "Alliance for Progress" to "Great Society" and "War on Poverty." "Just Society" and Ronald

Reagan's "Creative Society" don't seem to have caught on. What new slogans are in store?

Bureaucratic coinages of the type of "Medicare," "Medi-caid," "Medical," have been joined by Mayor Lindsay's ineffable "Urbanaid," and Eugene Nickerson's "Localaid," which differs from the former in demanding federal aid for all localities, not merely the big, slum-infested cities. The formation of these words is crystal-clear, even if the way they operate is not (Medical is the California version of the Medi-caid phenomenon), and etymologies won't be necessary. The recent creation of all these edifying terms is attested by the fact that none of them appears in our most recent and com-prehensive dictionaries, with the single exception of Medicare, which comes to light only in the 1966 Random House Dictionary, with a definition that may be summarized as "com-prehensive medical care sponsored by government." (Social-ized or State Medicine was the earlier term.) In all these expressions there is the image of a benevolent, beneficent Welfare State, coupled with the implication of something for nothing. "Urbanaid" further establishes a link with the made-to-order fiscal problems of the cities, and how to get both federal and state governments involved in them.

"Charisma" is another lovely word, far from new, which we have seen applied to such popular leaders as the late Senator Robert Kennedy. It is of Biblical Greek origin, and the Oxford Dictionary traces its use in English back to 1641, but in the form "Charism," and with the meaning of "favor vouchsafed by God," "grace," "talent." Even the 1961 Web-ster's Third gives it in the sense of "supernatural effluvium," stressing its divine origin. But the later Random House Dic-tionary carries the definition on to "special spiritual power or personal quality which gives an individual authority or influence over many." The second part of this would seem to cover the Kennedy case adequately. The charismatic quality may also be exercised by virtue of one's office, which would conceivably take in anything from Pope Paul and

Billy Graham to Adam Clayton Powell. But aside from this "charisma" is a good tool for placing halos around the head of politicians.

In the Alice-in-Wonderland realm of taxation, three weasel terms, not necessarily new, but certainly overused, seem to predominate: "broad-based," "ability to pay," "fairest." The first is heard in the case of states, like New Jersey, which had long held out against tax-and-spendomania, allowing excises bridge and road tolls, and real estate taxes to supply them with the bulk of their revenue. (These, be it noted, are all forms of taxation where you pay for what you get and get what you pay for.) The "broad-based" tax is a euphemism for the kind of tax that hits everybody, regardless of whether he gets anything back or not. The term is accurate only to a degree. Certainly the sales tax hits everybody, roughly in proportion to what he consumes; but so do excises, road tolls, and real estate taxes. All these forms of taxation have in common the characteristic that the taxpayer has some measure of control over them insofar as they affect him. He doesn't have to smoke, drink alcoholic beverages, or buy gasoline; he can take alternate routes, save when he crosses rivers; he does not have to own real estate; and he can limit his consumption of taxable articles. The income tax is different. There is no way of legally avoiding it save to have no income, and that, for most people, would mean starvation. It is in connection with the income tax that we get the other two slogans. It is said to be, by such experts as Governor Hughes of New Jersey and Mayor Lindsay of New York City, the "fairest type of tax" because it is based on "ability to pay." These two claims are swallowed, along with the tax, without thought or protest.

"Fairest" to whom? Here we are reminded of the "unfair" that so often appears on labor-union picket signs, which is discussed elsewhere in this book. What is "fair" about a type of taxation that promotes indolence and penalizes initiative and success? It may be "fair" in the eyes of Lenin, who advocated a steeply progressive income tax as one of the devices whereby non-Communist regimes could be weakened and overthrown. As for "ability to pay," if two friends, one of whom makes $100, the other $300 a week, are in the habit of going out together, the "ability to pay" formula would prescribe that the wealthier of the two should invariably foot the bill. This might even offend his friend's self-respect. There was an earlier formula, current in the first decades of this century, which at least had the merit of being brutally frank: "Soak the rich!" But the steeply progressive income tax, as we now know it, strikes all the way down to the $600-a-year income. "Progressive" is itself a weasel word, since it means "steeply graduated" to hit higher incomes, but has overtones of "progress." By using the twin formulas of "ability to pay" and "fairest tax," we are in a fair way to achieving confiscation, since every taxing authority, federal, state, and city, fastens on the same income, and calls it "fair."

But taxation can also work in reverse. Here is a proposal, supported by at least one 1968 presidential candidate, Senator Eugene McCarthy, for what is euphemistically known as a "negative tax," or "guaranteed minimum annual income plan." The idea figures prominently in Galbraith's *The Affluent Society*, but it seems to have originated in 1962 with Milton Friedman, a conservative economist, who proposed replacing the welfare bureaucracy with a graduated scale of payments made by the government to the individual, and based on a reversal of the current income tax and deduction system. Estimates of how much it would cost range from 11 to 26 billion dollars a year, as against the current eight-billion-dollar welfare bill.

The plan, in modified form, has been tried out in Massachusetts on the state level, with debatable results, due to the difficulty of constructing an income tax return that would supply all the information pertinent to the allowance of the credit, as well as of checking on the authenticity of that information.

There may or may not be merit to this plan, which would, at least in theory, abolish the odium and humiliation of relief and welfare handouts. If Gallup Polls mean anything, it is interesting that only 36 per cent of the general population is for this plan, with 58 per cent against. The figures for non-whites, however, are 66 per cent for, 30 per cent against; but families with incomes below $3,000 a year, including all racial groups, show 48 per cent for to 45 per cent against. The identical voters, on being asked for their reactions to a guaranteed work plan (this would amount to making the government the employer of last resort), come out with an astounding 78 per cent for to 18 per cent against. Here non-whites are even more overwhelming in their desire for work: 86 per cent for to 13 per cent against; while families with incomes below $3,000 show 83 per cent for to 16 per cent against. Apparently, low income groups, black or white, prefer the assurance of a job to a guaranteed income.

On the linguistic side, the idea is so recent that none of our dictionaries offers "guaranteed minimum (annual) income," though "guaranteed annual wage," an earlier darling of the labor unions, is reported by both Webster's Third and the Random House Dictionary. "Negative tax," which appears nowhere, has rare weasely features. Both its component parts go back to Middle English. The word "negative," which is the real kernel of the expression, is defined in the sense of "denial, refusal, veto, negation, absence of," but nowhere does it appear in the sense in which it is used in the compound (a tax paid by the government to the "taxpayer"). The Random House Dictionary, in its more comprehensive definition, says that "negative" is "lacking in positive attributes; lacking in constructiveness, optimism, or helpfulness," and this definition, though not specifically created or applied, seems to cover the situation quite well.

CHAPTER 12

The Language of Foreign Relations and Foreign Aid

The language of foreign relations of an earlier day is replete with semantic gems. "Entangling Alliances" goes all the way back to Washington and Jefferson, "Isolationism" and "War to End War" to Wilsonian times. The Oxford Dictionary informs us that as far back as 1911 we had the expression "self-determination," later amplified by Wilson into "self-determination for small nations," a slogan that was used to fragment central Europe into a conglomeration of weak states unable to stand on their own feet, which proved an easy prey, first for the Nazis, later for the Communists. "Open covenants openly arrived at" is still another Wilsonian coinage. "Peace in our time" was the attractive package that Neville Chamberlain sold to the people of Great Britain after Munich, with the result that those same peace-loving Britons had to face, a very short time later, war and its horrors. "Munich" became a by-word at that time, and even "Municheer" was coined to describe Chamberlain's followers. "Unconditional surrender" led to the prolongation of World War II and the Communist takeover of eastern Europe and large slices of the Far East. "Bring the boys home!" meant that we could not win the peace after having won the war. But before that we had heard FDR's dulcet tones assuring us "a-gain and a-gain and a-gain" that our boys would never be sent overseas.

More recently we have had such expressions as "cold war," said to have been coined by H. B. Swope. Its appearance in the 1932 Oxford Dictionary is no doubt due to the revision made in 1950, where it is properly defined as a state of hostility involving threats, propaganda, and obstructive tactics, but no actual violence. The Random House Dictionary practically equates it to "war of nerves." One commentator reflects upon the term with the remark that one is uncertain whether we should wish for the temperature to go up, in which case we get a hot, or shooting war, or down, sending us into the deep freeze in our relations with the Soviets. "Positions (or "situations") of strength" is attributed to Dean Acheson, while "brinkmanship" apparently started with a satirical buildup on Secretary Dulles' statement about going to the very brink of war. ("Gapsmanship" is a more recent newspaper coinage.) "Containment," first suggested by George Kennan, started even earlier.

All these expressions have their legitimate uses, whatever one may think of the practices or conditions they describe. At the most weasely, they may be cited in a spirit of irony or sarcasm.

But there is also an entire series of expressions, some old, some new, which betray interesting states of mind, like Wilson's "He kept us out of war," "Wilson's wisdom wins without war," and "too proud to fight," which didn't last long, or Eisenhower's "waging peace," which we are still trying to do. Then there are such terms as "disarmament" and "armament reduction," "multilateral treaty," "non-aggression" (this is a favorite with the Soviets, particularly when followed by "pact"), "collective security," "surrender of sovereignty," "peaceful coexistence" (another Soviet term, coined in 1922, but used in English since 1954, and subject to various definitions, depending on who is the Soviet spokesman at the moment), "summit" ("meetings at the summit" began with Churchill, while Sorensen gave us the elegant derivative "summitry"). "Nuclear proliferation," which both we and the Soviets are trying to stop, appears as a 1949 Adlai Stevenson coinage. There is a "people-to-people" formula, sponsored by Eisenhower, which overlooks the fact that it is impossible for people to get at other people who live under dictatorial forms of government, because the government won't allow it. (This is a bit like the man who couldn't keep his appointment at the church with his bride-to-be because his wife wouldn't let him.)

There are "negotiations," "unconditional," as in the Johnson formula, or conditioned upon acceptance and compliance by the other side, as in the view favored by the military. "Negotiate" goes back to Latin *negotium*, which is compounded of *nec* and *otium* ("not" plus "leisure"; in other words, "activity," "business"). It has been used since 1599 in the sense of "to hold intercourse with a view to coming to terms," "to confer regarding a basis of agreement between two contending parties." The noun "negotiation" is twenty years older than the verb, at least so far as recorded appearance is concerned. The word is quite harmless, but its application in modern times and in the field of international relations has given it sinister overtones. In the acceptance of liberators like Nehru, Sukarno, Khrushchev, and Ho Chi Minh, "I want to negotiate with you about Goa, West Irian, Berlin, or South Vietnam" really means: "I want to tell you what I want, and you had better come across, or else!" The late *Untouchables* television program never thought of having its Frank Nitti or Al Capone character tell a speakeasy owner marked out for a shakedown: "Let's negotiate!" but it ought to have taken advantage of the opportunity. In our recent foreign policy, or what passes for such, we have a new definition for "negotiations," as exemplified by the Paris talks with the North Vietnamese. "Negotiations" is what goes on while we draw back from some of our military activities, such as the bombing of Hanoi, while the enemy expands his (the rocket bombing of Saigon). In the face of this, we have a call for further negotiations, preceded by a complete stoppage of our bombing. Would not complete withdrawal be simpler, if surrender to an enemy who won't negotiate in good faith is what is really desired? Humphrey's "cease fire" proposal is of a similar nature. It takes two to cease fire, unless the proposition is meant to set up Americans as fireless sitting ducks for the North Vietnamese and Viet Cong. What comes to mind is Truman's now famous saying: "If you can't stand the heat, get out of the kitchen!"

One might also mention a few additional terms that have on occasion been used in the course of the Vietnam war. "Antennae" and "feelers" have been described as what the two sides use when one wants to find out how the other feels about the matter of negotiations, and "tunnel" as the long pull of what started out as a short, easy war. "Signals" is described as a method of letting the other side know our intentions without telling them in plain words, which they would not believe.

Then there are those two popular terms, "hawks" and "doves." The first seems to have been put into circulation by Senator Fulbright, though "war hawks" goes back to Jefferson. All three of our dictionaries offer the use of "hawk" as applied to a person, but only in the sense of one who preys on others, especially a swindler. "Dove," as a symbol of peace, goes all the way back to Noah's Ark and Greek mythology (the doves of Aphrodite). The Oxford Dictionary, rather strangely, does not offer it as applied to a person; both Webster's Third and the Random House Dictionary do, but in the sense of a pure, innocent, gentle, tender person, especially a woman or child. The current use of "hawk" as a Vietnam warmonger and of "dove" as a Vietnam appeaser appears in none of the dictionaries. "Settlement is the name of the game," used by McGeorge Bundy in 1966, gave us a saying that has become very popular.

Side by side with the terminology of the Vietnam war runs that of accommodation with the guiding spirit and supplier of North Vietnam and the Viet Cong, the USSR. Here two expressions of long standing have recently come to the fore.

They are "building bridges to" and "the spirit of something or other."

"Building bridges," a favorite term with President Johnson and his State Department, was regularly rounded out to "building bridges to the Communist countries" or "to the Soviet Union." The implication was that we are trying to get closer to those nations through trade and cultural and diplomatic relations. This could perhaps be accepted as a national policy were it not for the fact that we are waging hostilities against other Communist nations, and the ones with which we trade in turn supply our enemies with deadly weapons to be used against us. Some of these arms are manufactured with materials supplied by us. The situation is reminiscent of our huge sales of scrap iron to Japan before World War II, and the use of that scrap in the bombs that hit us at Pearl Harbor. But on that occasion there was at least a time lag between our supplying our potential enemies and their ultimate use of what we supplied. Here the two processes are simultaneous. Logic would demand that you either build bridges or blast them.

The "Spirit of" bit, in its diplomatic application, first came to our notice in Eisenhower's "Spirit of Camp David," where there was friendly entertainment of then Premier Khrushchev. The Spirit blew apart when the Soviets discovered that we were spying on them via U-2 planes. More recently we have had the "Spirit of Glassboro" or "Hollybush" (satirized by some wit into the "Spirit of Quackenbush" after the name of a character in a Marx Brothers comedy). Here the circumstances were that Premier Kosygin had come to the United States for the sole purpose of making strongly anti-American speeches in the United Nations Assembly. It was seen fit to extend to him the hospitality of the nation's President, the Governor and State of New Jersey, and Glassboro College, which at least proved that we had not forgotten the rules of courtesy. Kosygin accepted the hospitality in non-committal fashion, though politely enough. It was observed, however, that upon his return to New York and the United Nations Assembly, his anti-American attitude was altogether unchanged. This doesn't mean too much, save that the incident was fastened upon by the appeasers in our midst as indicative of what a "soft" approach could accomplish. Actually, it accomplished nothing, although some Glassboro residents traveled to Russia to try to convince the Russians that we are human, something the Russians were probably aware of even before. So the "Spirit of Quackenbush" went to join the earlier "Spirit of Camp David," despite all optimistic editorials and wishful thinking. The confrontation between the West and the Communist world still stands. It may be remarked in passing that the only definition of "spirit" that seems to fit this peculiar American manifestation ("The Spirit of ——") is the one given by the Oxford Dictionary as "disposition" or "prevailing tone," by Webster's Third as "special attitude or frame of mind characterizing individuals or groups," and by the Random House Dictionary as "dominant tendency." The precise application of the term in the fashion described above appears nowhere in the dictionaries (closest example given is Shelley's "The spirit of the age"). "The Spirit of Old Siwash" is, of course, traditional in academic circles. There is a further precedent, not cited by the dictionaries, in the 1876 painting entitled "The Spirit of '76." But it's not quite the same thing.

Lastly, we might mention the rash of new political creations in -*ism* ("Maoism," "Castroism," "Guevarism," etc.), built up on the analogy of such earlier coinages as "Titoism," and designed to illustrate the various faces of the enemy that wants to bury us. The remote implication that is supposed to be fostered in our minds is that there is a difference in the ultimate goal of the various brands of Communism. There isn't.

But it would be a grievous mistake to suppose that our

foreign relations vocabulary ends where the Communist world begins. Franklin Roosevelt's "Good Neighbor Policy" long antedates Kennedy's "Alliance for Progress." So does Willkie's "One World."

There is an entire set of weasel words that are meant to justify our "global commitments" (a State Department favorite) with relation not merely to common defense, but to the vast program of economic aid that has cost us many billions of dollars with somewhat debatable results. It was as far back as 1942 that Clare Boothe Luce coined the term "globaloney," surprisingly mentioned in none of our dictionaries, to describe Henry Wallace's plan to "deliver a bottle of milk on the doorstep of every Hottentot."

Consider, for instance, what former Secretary of Agriculture Orville Freeman used to call "concessional exports." These are exports of grain and other agricultural commodities to countries that never pay for them. These "concessional exports," which have finally turned our huge farm surpluses into shortages, go into official figures on imports and exports at their full dollar value, causing taxpayers to wonder how there can be a drain upon our gold stocks when our exports are so much higher than our imports. Historically, the root word "concession" first appears in 1611 as a synonym for "grant," adding the meaning of "something conceded" in 1647. "Concessional," not reported by the Oxford Dictionary, appears in Webster's Third as "granted," "conceded," "yielding to request, pressure, claim or demand," which about tells the story. An earlier, more justifiable variant of "concessional exports" was World War II's "lease-lend" (1941).

Long before the coining of "concessional exports," an entire glossary of words had arisen to describe the recipients of our bounty, actual and proposed. "Develop" is a thoroughly legitimate word that ultimately goes back to Latin *dis* and *volvere* ("to un-roll, un-fold"). But much can be done by compounding, and "underdeveloped" is an illustration, having been surrounded with a halo of associations and implications.

"Underdeveloped" does not appear in the older Webster's or the Oxford Dictionary, but the 1961 Webster's Third defines it as "failing to realize a potential economic level and standard of living because of lack of capital, shortage of trained technicians, medical assistance, or" (and for this we bless the compilers) "culture traits resistant to change." It is only the last alternative that removes the odium from us and puts it on the underdeveloped themselves. All other clauses imply that the state of anybody being underdeveloped is basically our fault. This, of course, goes hand in hand with the view so often expressed that it is not merely our pleasure and privilege, but our duty to help the underdeveloped. Our help is vociferously demanded, at least by the leaders of the underdeveloped nations; whether their populations are invariably willing and ready to accept it is a somewhat different story, and here we have an escape hatch. The use of "underdeveloped" is a clue to a state of mind, that of the international do-gooders. As a suitable substitute we should suggest "backward," which at least is non-committal as to whose is the responsibility for deplorable states of affairs. Both "underdeveloped" and "backward," however, have by this time been invested with the connotation that it's all our fault if these nations refuse to apply modern methods to their agricultural production and sacred cows, or population control to their exuberant production of more mouths to feed.

"Have-not" nations, more frank, is a term first coined by Cervantes, though he applied it to persons rather than countries. A recent replacement, appearing in a *Newark Star-Ledger* editorial, is "haveless," but it goes back to Middle English. More euphemistic are "fledgling nations" (this was Eleanor Roosevelt's creation), more recently replaced by "emergent" or "emerging nations" (emerging from what, one might ask?). "Uncommitted," "unaligned," and "neutralist" are splendid terms to apply to these nations when they sponge on both us and our enemies.

Other curious linguistic phenomena have appeared in recent times that betoken America's penitent mood with respect to "emergent" nations. Consider "Asian," as against the "Asiatic" of our younger days. For some time, we had been noting that "Asian" was becoming more and more current, while "Asiatic," practically in universal use down to World War II, was being used more and more seldom, more and more reluctantly. "Afro-Asiatic" is practically never used (it does appear in connection with languages in Webster's Third); it's always "Afro-Asian." We made inquiries. "Asiatic," we were told, had taken on offensive connotations. Why? No one knew. Both words come down straight from Greek (*Asianos, Asiatikos*). "Asian," if anything, is the older word in English; its first recorded appearance is in 1563, while "Asiatic" appears only in 1631, and then with application to literary style rather than to people. The *-atic* suffix is in itself harmless; of Greek origin (*-atikos*), it means "of the kind of"; it appears in such scientific or semi-scientific adjectives as "automatic," "lymphatic," "chromatic," "axiomatic," as well as in geographical connotations ("Adriatic," "Hanseatic"). Earlier dictionaries, including the Oxford, give both terms and make no reference to offensive connotations. But the 1961 Webster's specifically states of "Asiatic": "now often taken to be offensive." Is this a self-inflicted wound on the part of the Asians? Did the Westerners utter the word "Asiatic" with such a grimace of disgust back in the ugly days of colonialism that the Asiatics, or Asians, got an inferiority complex? But above all, should we go along with the new usage, and avoid "Asiatic"? For myself, I claim the right to go on using it, without intent to offend, as I have always done. "Asia," by the way, was a term originally applied only to what we know today as Asia Minor. The best bet is that it comes from Assyrian *Asu*, "the East," as opposed to *Ereb*, "the West," which may have given us "Europe." The twain have met at last, in the United Nations circles.

Before leaving the international field, it may be worth while to cast a glance at an item that is not properly a weasel word, but rather a misnomer due to a widespread misconception of the same class as that which led early explorers to describe the natives of the Western Hemisphere as "Indians." At the time of the appearance of the novel *The Ugly American*, the title described a character who, while physically unprepossessing, was morally lovable and tremendously helpful to the native population of a southeastern Asian country. People who had not read the novel but thought they knew what the title meant began to use "Ugly American" in the sense of an American who goes to a foreign land to exploit it and throw his weight around, making both himself and his nation objects of scorn and execration. As is usual in these cases (note how Capri is now universally stressed on the last syllable because it suited a song writer to make it rhyme with "me" at the end of a verse), corrections were worse than useless. "Ugly American" stands today as a perennial monument to folk-misinterpretation, standing in the popular mind for all that is unlovely and unwise in our dealings with other countries. There is no mention of "Ugly American" in any of our dictionaries, however.

CHAPTER 13

The Voice of Annihilation

The vocabulary of war is as old as war itself. Here, we can accumulate a fine hoard of weasel words, some designed to fool the enemy, but most of them elaborated for our own consumption. There is Theodore Roosevelt's "Big Stick," which goes back to the very beginning of this century, but has been superseded by the updated "deterrent," in use since 1829, but very recently revived as a military expression. "Task force" and "Operation-something-or-other" (as distinguished from the earlier "military operation") seem to have arisen in the course of World War II, which also gave us the weasely "liberation" for "invasion," thought up by an editor of the *Richmond News-Leader* and enthusiastically approved by President Roosevelt, who knew the value of a slogan when he saw one, to describe what was about to happen to Europe without unduly hurting the feelings of the Europeans, who after taking the Nazi occupation were now about to be required to take the Anglo-American bombings. It was the same FDR who coined two of the finest slogans of that war, "Stab in the Back," to refer to Mussolini's declaration of war on France after France was down, and "Day of Infamy," to describe Japan's sneak attack on Pearl Harbor. Earlier in the conflict we had had the expression "Phony War" to describe Franco-British inaction through the winter of 1939-1940, while Poland and Finland were being brutalized by the Nazis and Communists.

"Arsenal of democracy," to describe America's role in supplying the materials of war for all Allied forces, was as lofty-sounding as "fraternization," "sororization," and "to liberate," used by the G.I.'s to describe their own questionable activities in occupied countries, were lowly. ("Fraternization" and "to fraternize" are old words, dating back to 1611; the military abbreviation "fratting" appears in 1945; "to sororize," given by the Oxford Dictionary as a "rare" word, goes back to 1875, but not in the sense in which it was used by the soldiers, "to be free and easy with the womenfolk of ally and enemy alike"; in fact, none of our dictionaries gives it in that sense; "to liberate," as a slangy euphemism for "to swipe," appears in both Webster's Third and the Random House Dictionary, though not in the Oxford Dictionary.)

One of the words favored by President Eisenhower, though he did not coin it, was "infrastructure," which can be used indifferently in a military or political sense, to describe an army's installations or a government's administrative apparatus. The Oxford Dictionary does not give it, and the Random House Dictionary offers it only as applied to the structure of NATO. "Crusade," a medieval word, used now and then to describe any movement with a high moral content, was resurrected by Eisenhower in connection with the military phase of the invasion of Europe, and later used in the title of his book *Crusade in Europe*.

"No substitute for victory" was offered by General Mac-Arthur at the time of the Korean war, in response to Dean Rusk's concept of "limited war" (maintaining peace and security without a general conflagration), a concept which has finally brought us to the present pass in Vietnam.

To a greater or lesser degree, all these expressions contain weasely features. None of them, however, can compare with another coinage of the Korean war, Truman's ineffable "Police Action," now thoroughly accepted by our modern American dictionaries in a general sense; or, better yet, with the verb "brainwash," which had been known since 1950, but became really popular when it began to happen to Americans who had been taken prisoner by the Chinese and North Koreans. The verb began to snowball, to the point where it could be used by Governor Romney at the outset of the 1968 campaign to describe what had been done to him by the military on his earlier visit to Vietnam. "Brainwash" appears in the older Oxford Dictionary, but only in the Addenda and as a colloquialism. Webster's Third describes it as a literal translation of the Chinese hsi^3 mao^3, "wash brain." "Forcible indoctrination" and "menticide" are among the synonyms given. Its application to internal democratic politics is exemplified by "to brainwash the voters." The Random House Dictionary goes into greater detail: "to change attitudes or beliefs through torture, drugs, or psychological devices, characteristic of controlled systems, and often based on repetition or confusion." The voters seemed reluctant to accept a candidate who admitted to having let himself be brainwashed, and the word that was meant to explain away some of the inconsistencies in Governor Romney's stand on the Vietnam war boomeranged badly. Nevertheless, we may now expect anyone who seeks an excuse for his actions to claim he was brainwashed, so that the expression superlatively qualifies for the role of weasel word.

The general vocabulary of modern warfare is replete with weaselry, mainly in the form of modest understatements. "Confrontation," however light-hearted or ominous it may sound, is legitimate enough. Its etymology has to do with two foreheads that touch (Latin *cum* plus *frons*, "with-forehead," almost like Secretary Rusk's "eyeball to eyeball"), and the verb "to confront," in the sense of to face in hostility or defiance, has been in active use since 1589.

To take a few expressions from our enemies, "transfer of populations" equals deportation, "rectification of frontiers" means annexation, "elimination of unreliable elements" is liquidation *en masse*. We, too, have our weasel words, starting with "Department of Defense," where once we had the more frank "Department of War." True, the present Department of Defense includes also the old Department of the Navy and the new and ebulliently aggressive Air Force; but is it not a euphemism to speak of "defense" when you are waging a war 10,000 miles from home? We call the North Vietnamese and Vietcong "aggressors"; they retaliate by using the same word on us. "Pacification" and "peace-keeping action," like the "Police Action" of Korea, seem at times to be rather loosely used when they involve destruction of villages and deportation of the inhabitants. What used to be (and still is, on television) a "Commando raid" when carried out by our side, becomes "terrorism" and "sneak attack" when committed by our opponents. "Retaliation" can mean almost anything. In military parlance, "strategic withdrawal" can be used to mean "rout," and "phased withdrawal" to mean "rout with insufficient means of transportation." It has been pointed out by more than one writer that the use of "American boys" instead of "American men" or "American troops" is a loaded term, designed to play on the emotions of parents. ("If we have to destroy all the monuments in Europe to save the life of a single American boy, let's do it!" ran a letter to a newspaper at the time of the bombing of the Monte Cassino Abbey.)

There is also in evidence the use of a form of Pentagonese whose main exemplifications lie in the field of atomic warfare, discussed a little farther on. But a few terms are unspecialized: "manpowerization," for instance, for which no dictionary offers justification; or "hardware," referring to major non-atomic weapons, which has gotten into the dictionaries, and to accompany which "software" has been borrowed from computer jargon, to indicate the organization and command-and-control arrangements that govern the use of the hardware. "Breakthrough," now used in so many diverse fields, is in origin a military loan-translation of German *Durchbruch*, which came to us in 1924. "Brass" for higher echelons of the military command, is an old word, from 1899; it was in origin "brass hat," and referred to the gold braid on officers' hats.

"Interdiction bombing" is described by the Oxford Dictionary as an American creation, to indicate the sort of aerial bombing that is designed to break up enemy transport and communications. "To liaise," a back-formation on "liaison," with the meaning of "to establish military communications," has been around long enough to get into the Oxford Dictionary's Addenda.

"To attrite," a word for the use of which Secretary of Defense McNamara was roundly criticized, is justified by the Random House Dictionary in the sense of "to make smaller by attrition," and appears as an adjective as early as 1625, with the alternate form "attrited," which presupposes a verbal use. There are euphemistic descriptions of weapons, which are invariably gentle understatements: "sophisticated," "anti-personnel," "conventional." The first, in use since 1603, has its root in Greek *sophia*, "skill," "wisdom," but also "cunning," "shrewdness." The earliest English use is in the sense of "altered, adulterated, falsified." Webster's Third goes on to add "complex" to "adulterated," while our truly sophisticated Random House Dictionary calls it "altered by education or experience, worldly-wise, not naive, complex or intricate." In connection with weapons, it is presumably the "complex," "intricate" definition that applies. (Sophisticated weapons are those the Russians have of late been supplying to the North Vietnamese and to the Egyptians, who used them to good effect on Israel's *Elath*.) "Anti-personnel," again appearing in the American dictionaries (but not in the Oxford Dictionary), refers to that which is meant to destroy or maim enemy personnel rather than such objects as trucks or buildings. "Anti-personnel weapon" is a sophisticated euphemism for "killer weapon." "Conventional," in use since 1583, referred at first to what is settled by convention, law, or contract, or is in accord with tradition. The American dictionaries define it as "sanctioned by agreement or usage," "conforming to standards or agreements." Nowhere is there reference to "conventional" in connection with weapons, though we all know that what is meant is weapons such as were used down to the end of World War II, not of the new atomic fission, ballistic, or space type. In accordance with the earlier definitions, however, even such weapons become conventional now that their production and use are governed by international agreements. (Or are they?)

Connected with the Vietnam conflict are two expressions, one of which, "selective draft," goes back quite a way, while the other, "credibility gap," is a 1965 creation. "Selective draft," or "selective service," in the military sense, has been in use since the early eighteenth century, and Webster's Third defines it as "the process of selecting people for compulsory military service." The basis of the selection differs from country to country and from system to system. The selective draft was not too long ago expanded to include graduate students in the universities, which may have had something to do with the growing sympathy for student riots, though the underlying causes of the latter were of another nature. It might nevertheless be suggested that for a war that is basically colonial, and not fought in direct defense of the homeland or the nation's existence, a professional force might be better suited than one composed of partly unwilling draftees.

"Credibility gap," a 1965 creation, betokens, in the eyes of the independent news media and the population at large, the difference between what you can and what you cannot believe in the news handouts of government agencies, particularly the Department of Defense. Safire claims that its first occurrence was in the form of a button sported by American soldiers in South Vietnam which read: "Ambushed at Credibility Gap." But he applies it more specifically to the statements of Lyndon Johnson, in the economic as well as the military field.

"Gradualism," a term far more often used in connection with civil rights, has one military use connected with escalation, another that links with negotiations. "Escalation" itself, a choice word of our foreign policy, is so recent that in its present acceptance the Oxford Dictionary does not have it at all, and the 1961 Webster has it only in the sense of "an increase in price to counteract an unjust discrepancy." "To escalate," likewise in Webster's Third, has only the meaning of "to carry up on a conveyor belt," bearing out the Oxford Dictionary's 1904 "escalator," given as a U.S. term for a moving stairway. The more recent 1966 Random House Dictionary, however, has "escalate" in the sense of "to increase in magnitude or intensity," exemplified with "to escalate a war." Safire traces this use of the word to Herman Kahn, a thermonuclear thinker who in the 1950s offered a sixteen-step "escalation ladder" by which we go from a disagreement to an all-out war. *Time* magazine, in April 1967, described "escalation" as "one of those windy words that are foisted upon the public by military bureaucrats, interminably parroted by the press, and kept in the vernacular long after losing any real meaning." This is at least as good a definition of a weasel word as the one offered by Theodore Roosevelt in the early years of this century.

Many terms of what Richard Lingeman calls "Vietlish" (a jargon developed out of our Vietnam experience) lend themselves to highly sarcastic treatment. "Alternative terminations," for instance, is a way out that no one has thought of yet. "Flexible response" is whatever means of fighting are available at the moment; but the term also has a loftier use to denote something short of all-out war in response to enemy aggression or provocation (our action, or inaction, in connection with the *Pueblo* incident, defined by Secretary of State Rusk as "intolerable," for instance). "Unconditional (or "permanent") bombing halt" is what the enemy would like, while "bombing pause" is what we are willing to concede. "The Other Side" is described as a portmanteau word coined by Secretary Rusk to include the Vietcong, the National Liberation Front, Hanoi, and even Red China, if we can get them to come in. "Defoliation," favored by Goldwater, means in Lingeman's concept "killing off all the hostile vegetation in a given area" (but the word "defoliation" has been legitimately used since 1793); while "peace offensive" has the double meaning of "diplomatic activity aimed at persuading The Other Side to engage in Unconditional Negotiations," and "Communist propaganda masking an intention to continue aggression."

Another writer defines "military advisors" (who preceded the use of combat forces) as American pilots who carry bombs and napalm for the destruction of Vietnamese villages, and inquires whether such an advisor has ever advised against dropping either.

One touch of comedy in the midst of tragedy is the abortive attempt to replace "napalm" (a telescoping of naphthene and palmitate, in use since 1942) with "naphthagel" and similar coinages. Perhaps it was thought that the students wouldn't demonstrate quite so loudly if Dow Chemical produced the same product by an unfamiliar designation. But a rose by any other name . . .

Far more of a nightmare than even the Vietnam war is the specter of full-fledged atomic warfare. This, curiously, has been receding into the background as the Vietnam hostilities unfolded, perhaps on the assumption that the latter proved that the first is not inevitable, even under provocation. Here we have such terms as "total war," not offered by our dictionaries, which goes back to Ludendorff's 1935 *Der Totale Krieg*, a type of war described as involving the destruction of the enemy's productive capacity, something that the coiner of the expression, at the time, could not envisage as carried out to the atomic conclusion of wiping out the foe's major cities with all their inhabitants. "Preventive war" (or "preemptive strike") is a devastating sneak attack on a potential foe before he is ready to launch an attack of his own; this has been advocated by many in connection with Red China, and, amazingly, by Bertrand Russell, of "Better Red than dead" fame, in 1948, in connection with Russia, which did not yet have a fully developed atom bomb. That the phrase need not be altogether equated with atomic or total war is shown by its use in connection with Israeli destructive attacks on the Arab forces that were preparing to wipe out Israel. "Massive retaliation" is John Foster Dulles' 1953 creation. "Missile gap" is the charge made by Kennedy in the 1960 campaign that the Eisenhower administration had lagged behind Soviet armament production—a very surprising charge, in view of the later policy of the Kennedy and Johnson administrations to bring ourselves down to the Soviet armament level so that the good Soviets should not suffer from an inferiority complex. It may be remarked in passing that this was a weasel usage of the finest coinage. (More recently, the Republicans retaliated with "megatonnage gap," to describe what had been going on under the Kennedy-Johnson-Rusk administration.) Then we have "atomic potential" and "atomic holocaust." The first, as nearly as we can make out (the group appears in no dictionary) indicates the resources at a nation's disposal for producing both atomic power and atomic (or hydrogen) bombs. The latter was a Kennedy favorite that replaced the earlier "missile gap" when we decided to go soft; "holocaust" is Greek for "completely burnt offering," and that is what President Kennedy said we would be turned into if war ever broke out with the Soviets. "Deterrence" (1861) is what earlier generations called "preparedness," the sort of thing designed to convince the ill-intentioned that they had better not start anything they couldn't finish; etymologically, it comes from Latin *de* plus *terreo*, "to frighten off." The dread "fallout," first coined in 1953 to indicate the radioactive particles that float down through the atmosphere after an atomic explosion and contaminate everything, has now become generalized to the point of serving many fields, notably the political, in the sense of "unfortunate or unexpected side effects."

"Destruct," which is used of missiles that miscarry or misfunction, does not appear in the Oxford Dictionary, but is given in the American dictionaries in the sense of "to destroy intentionally." It is further described as a back-formation from the noun "destruction." Since it is seldom that one destroys unintentionally, we still wonder whether it is not superfluous in the language. "Destruct" may also be used as an adjective, as in "a missile equipped with an autodestruct mechanism."

Our military authorities, and the anti-militarists who oppose them, have brought into common use such terms as "overkill" and "fail-safe," which no dictionary offers. Safire attributes the first to Herman Kahn (1960), with the meaning of "more nuclear destruction than is needed to wipe out the enemy's entire population," and describes the second as a system whereby a retaliatory strike can be recalled if the original signal was a mistake; if the bombers "fail" to receive confirmation, they return home, placing the communications failure on the "safe" side. Along with these are such terms as "city bargaining" ("you spare Chicago and we'll spare Leningrad"), and "unacceptable damage," meaning what a country cannot take in the way of atomic bombardment, leading to a surrender which might even work if there were anybody left to surrender or to surrender to. These word groups do not appear in our dictionaries, but "acceptable" goes back to 1380 with the meaning of "pleasing," "welcome," while the recent Webster's Third defines it as "capable or worthy of being accepted," and also "barely satisfactory or adequate," a strange meaning if you try to apply it to its opposite in a military sense. "To accept" is "to receive with consent," "to take without protest," and "to be able to take," which probably justifies the Pentagon in its use of "unacceptable." "Termination capability" and "survivability" are two more euphemisms of the military. The former (capacity to bring a war to a close) does not appear in Webster's Third; the second (ability to survive a full-scale modern war) does.

This chapter would hardly be complete without reference to the vocabulary of security and security clearance. "Security" is formed on Latin *securus* (free from care or worry); the question in connection with security is, of course, "security for whom and from what?"

The four degrees of security for military secrets and documents, of which only the first three appear in our American dictionaries, are: "restricted," which means not intended for general circulation; "classified," for circulation only in a given group; "top secret," which means that only a few high-placed individuals have access to the material; and "eyes only," meant for only one person to see (some doubt attaches to the authenticity of the last coinage). No special weasely connotations attach to the words themselves, but they can on occasion be misused. It has been charged that there is a tendency to attach these labels to materials, documents, processes, and even places to which the general public, including potential spies, have full and uncontested access, and that much material so labeled has no security importance whatsoever. "Classified" appears in the Oxford Dictionary only in a general, not in a military sense.

To what degree shall we take all this military jargon seriously? There is no doubt that the subject matter has very serious applications for all of us.

To what degree is it meant to confuse? Weasel words in some fields (education, advertising, economics) are, as a rule, gross overstatements. In the field of mass destruction, the tendency to understate and minimize the implications of the concepts involved is equally in evidence. This is natural. Total war means total annihilation, and no one likes the prospect of being annihilated. Those who deal in annihilation must therefore undersell, not oversell, their commodity, which in the final analysis is death. Can death's pill be sugar-coated? Apparently some think it can.

CHAPTER 14

Thunder on the Right

It is perhaps quite true that the political right does not possess or use anything like the arsenal of obloquy of the American left or of the Communist world. What is overlooked is that the vocabulary of the right is to a considerable degree an old, established, traditional vocabulary to which the older generation is thoroughly accustomed, and which does not arouse great controversy or even special attention. Also, there are many terms that can be used indifferently by both sides. It is the context, the facial expression (smile or sneer?), and the tone of voice that give the word semantic content. "Rugged individualism" can be a term of praise or one of irony; so can "liberal" or "progressive" or "conservative." So can "John Birch Society" on the one side, "Americans for Democratic Action" on the other. A good many of the right-wing terms are more economic than political in nature ("People's Capitalism," "American standard of living"), and will be discussed under the economic heading. Lastly, there are myriads of words and expressions of local pride and local patriotism, which may perhaps be viewed as rightist, but only occasionally lend themselves to purposes of weaselry ("Green Mountain Boys," "Keystone State," "Mother of Presidents," "Lone Star State," "Land of Enchantment," "Dark and Bloody Ground," "Dixie").

Among the more widespread and less objectionable right-wing terms are many that contain the words "America" or "American" ("American system," "American heritage," "American dream"). "American way of life" has even inspired a book titled *The American Way of Death;* while "Americanism," used since 1794 to betoken something peculiar to our country, particularly a language feature, and since 1808 in a patriotic sense, has given rise to an ironical "Americanitis," probably of British coinage. "America the Beautiful" is the title of a song to which few object, but "America First" was the name of an isolationistic group formed in the early 1940s to keep us out of world entanglements.

One of the best weasel words on record, in the sense that the meaning has been sucked right out of it, is "un-American." On the face of it, "un-American" should mean "not American," not "anti-American," which is the sense in which it is ordinarily used. Any foreign country legitimately carries on "un-American activities," which need not at all be directed against us. The term was first used in 1844 in connection with the Know-Nothing movement, which also described itself as "American." (It was that only in the sense that it was, among other things, anti-foreign.) A newspaper editorial of the period stated that the Know-Nothings, far from being "American," were "un-American." Though the word was kicked around for a long time, in all sorts of connotations, it was not until much later that it was picked up by a Congressional committee that used it in the sense of "radical," "subversive," "anti-national." Despite all expostulations, the connotation stuck and became generalized.

Side by side with "American," another adjective marches on, "Yankee." This is a word of highly doubtful origin and meaning. The Oxford Dictionary informs us that it appeared as early as 1683, being in use among the New York Dutch as a nickname, and this has led to the supposition that it may have been formed from *Jan Kees,* "John Cheese," a nickname applied by the Dutch to the English settlers. Another hypothesis is that it represents an American Indian mispronunciation of "English." Applied at first to English settlers in the northern colonies, particularly New England, the word was applied in the South to all Northerners, often with the prefix "damn-" before it; but Europeans transferred it to Americans in general, with the powerful help of George M. Cohan's *The Yanks Are Coming* at the time of World War I. Its most weasely use is in connection with laudatory nouns: "Yankee ingenuity," "Yankee inventiveness," "Yankee enterprise," "Yankee shrewdness," "Yankee know-how." ("Know-how," by the way, is of U.S. origin, and goes back to 1857, though some purists criticize it even today.) When used in this fashion, a strong nationalistic aura attaches to "Yankee," with the implication that Americans are more enterprising and know how to do things better than any other nation on earth, which is only partly true.

Overtones are often attached to the word "liberty," which again is made an American prerogative ("Liberty Bell," "liberty bonds," "liberty ships"). From the same "free" root of Latin comes the interesting "libertarian," often used by right-wing intellectuals to imply that they believe in freedom of the individual from government, at the same time that they disassociate themselves from "Liberals," a word that left-wing intellectuals have twisted far, far out of its original meaning. This enforced use of "libertarian" might be styled "weaselry by compulsion." The original use of "libertarian" was in philosophy and theology, to betoken a believer in the doctrine of free will as opposed to "necessitarian," one who believes in predestination, and in this sense the word appears in 1789; its political use, surprisingly, goes back to 1878, when "liberal" had already begun to slip.

There is a symbolism involved in the various names bestowed by patriotic Americans upon their flag. "Red, White, and Blue" and "Stars and Stripes" are in the main descriptive, but "Star-Spangled Banner" is poetic, and indeed goes back to the words of Francis Scott Key's song, which later turned into a national anthem, over the protests of pacifists who did not like the rockets' red glare and the bombs bursting in air. The origin of the term "Old Glory" can only be described as

closely guarded secret, at least so far as our major sources
are concerned. It does not appear in the British Oxford Dictionary. Webster's Third fails to give it by itself, though it
defines "Old Glory red" and "Old Glory blue" as colors. The
Random House Dictionary refers you to "Stars and Stripes,"
but when you turn to that entry there is no mention of Old
Glory. Other numerous dictionaries and encyclopedias at our
disposal remain discreetly silent. Perhaps one of our readers
will be kind enough to enlighten us as to the origin of the
term. Who coined it? When? Under what circumstances?

An American right-wing slogan that antedates Britain's
"White Man's Burden," coined by Kipling in 1899, is "Mani-
fest Destiny," said to go back to Andrew Jackson; the phrase
refers to the mission of the United States to expand from
ocean to ocean and beyond. Other expressions of reverence
for rightists, occasionally satirized by leftists, are "Pilgrim
Fathers" and "Founding Fathers," the first referring to the
seventeenth-century founders of the Massachusetts Bay Col-
ony, the second to the framers of the Declaration of Independence and the American Constitution, themselves the
objects of considerable reverence save to the generally ir-
reverent. Reference to the "Pilgrim Fathers" usually involves
an appeal to the moral virtues of an earlier era; reference to
the "Founding Fathers" usually involves principles of government and statements of human rights which the present day
sometimes forgets in its breathless search for civil rights. The
"Daughters of the American Revolution," otherwise known as
the DAR, founded in 1890 and including women who can
trace their ancestry back to participants in the American Revolution (on the right side; otherwise, apply for admission to
the Colonial Dames), often becomes a linguistic shibboleth,
as a paragon of old American virtues for the right, as a symbol
of racial and social intolerance for the left.

Other expressions current with rightists and derided by
leftists are as much economic as they are political: the afore-
mentioned "rugged individualism," attributed to Hoover in

the 1928 campaign, but disclaimed by him; "economic opportunity," "free competition," "free enterprise" (but this is a British creation from 1890, though it was abundantly used by such American Presidents as Wilson and Franklin D. Roosevelt); and the recently coined "people's capitalism," to betoken what we have been able to accomplish in the way of extending economic blessings to something like two-thirds of our population. Two dangers attach to this term: the other, more or less forgotten one-third, which at times becomes quite vocal, as shown by riots and Poor People's Marches; and the fact that "People's" has been largely preempted by the Communist world, which regularly labels its totalitarian regimes "People's Republics" or, better yet, "People's Democratic Republics."

On the derogatory side, the vocabulary of the right runs all the way from terms that are critical of administrations that are leftist but still within the tolerant framework of the traditional American two-party system, to words and expressions applied to Communism and Communists on the international front. In between lie those words and expressions which are used to belabor those among us who have Communist or Socialist sympathies.

"Statism," "paternalism," and "Welfare State" are three fairly mild and legitimate terms. The first seems rather recent, and the Oxford Dictionary does not show it. "Paternalism," on the other hand, goes back to 1881, but is far more generic, and used in other fields besides politics. "Welfare State" is a British coinage of 1948, enthusiastically accepted by right-wingers of both countries for purposes of criticism. All three are characteristic of what right-wingers often call "Big Government," a term coined on the older "Big Business" and often flanked by "Big Labor." (Only "Big Business" has recognition in our dictionaries.) The earmark of this system is what is sneeringly referred to as "cradle-to-grave" security, in the sense that the big, universal, paternal welfare state swallows up in taxes practically all of the individual's disposable income, but gives him in return such benefits as nationalized medicine and hospitalization (otherwise known as Medicare and Medicaid), job and unemployment insurance, Social Security, relief and welfare subsidies for those unable or unwilling to work, even funerals at government expense. This happy state of affairs is superlatively characteristic of Communist nations and, in modified form, of socialistically inclined states—e.g., Sweden, Finland, to some extent Great Britain; it is all a matter of degree rather than of basic principle. The Welfare State building up in America is therefore, in the right-wing view, a step in the march to socialism, which is itself another step in the march to Communism, defined as full government ownership and operation of all means of production and distribution and the abolition of private ownership of productive property and, as a corollary, of private enterprise and private employment. As the Welfare State develops, we have the unfolding of "spiraling inflation," "oppressive taxation," and "creeping socialism." (The last term was described, in the days of Franklin D. Roosevelt, as the hallmark of Old Guard Republicanism.) The terms "socialism" and "Communism" themselves go back to the 1830s and 1840s respectively, when Marx and Engels flourished, wrote, and preached. The distinction between socialism and Communism is largely a made-to-order one of the capitalistic world, and is not made by Marx or by the present-day Communist countries. (The Soviet Union officially defines itself as the Union of Socialist Soviet Republics.) The Western distinction lies in the methodology by which the socialist or Communist paradise is to be achieved, with the socialists advocating non-violent, parliamentary change, and the Communists favoring violent overthrow of capitalistic forms of government. In the 1964 campaign, a popular California poster reminded the voters that "Socialism is Communism," and to this some left-wingers took violent exception. It does seem, however, as though the supreme authority of the USSR might be acceptable in this matter, since it is the first country in which a fully socialistic (or Communistic) society has been achieved, at least in theory.

Other choice epithets range all the way from "crackpot" and "do-gooder" to "Brain Trust" and "Eastern Establishment." But "crackpot" is an all-purpose word, and while it may be applied to extremists of the left whose ideas are impractical, it can be equally applied to extreme right-wingers. "Do-gooder," strangely, is not a modern creation, but goes all the way back to 1654, with the possibility that it may have been borrowed by English as a loan-translation from the name of a medieval Italian semi-monastic order, the *Fate Bene Fratelli*, or "Do-Good Brothers." "Brain Trust" was coined by Raymond Moley, who formed part of the original organization, to designate that group of intellectuals who in 1933 volunteered to help and advise Roosevelt in his program of economic and social reform. Moley also coined a synonym on the analogy of "Commissariat": "Professoriat." In the popular mind there is an occasional, though erroneous, link between "Brain Trust" and "crackpot."

"Eastern Establishment" is a rather vague term loosely used to describe a group, located in the Northeast, and particularly in New York City, which is said to exercise a good deal of influence in determining both our internal and our foreign policies, mostly in a leftish direction. This group, if it really exists, is said to include some of our biggest foundations (particularly the Ford, Rockefeller, and Carnegie), *The New York Times*, and the Council on Foreign Relations, which has a roster of imposing names in its membership. The objective existence of the Eastern Establishment, or its operation as a concerted unit rather than as independent groups of like-minded persons and organizations, has never really been proved. But the "Eastern Establishment" supplies a most convenient whipping-boy when things go badly for the right.

Two additional specific terms directed against individuals are "the mess in Washington," which arose at the time of

Truman and was used, but not to sufficient avail, by Dewey, and "Government by croneyism," aimed at Lyndon Johnson's proclivity for appointing too many personal friends to highly responsible positions (Supreme Court justices, for instance). "Croneyism" is given only by the Random House Dictionary, the most recent of our dictionaries, but "crony" (or "croney") goes back to 1630. The Oxford Dictionary prefers to view it as an outgrowth of "crone" ("old hag"), which goes back to French *carogne*, "carrion," while Webster's Third prefers to link it to Greek *chronos*, "time" ("a friend from old times"), and offers as proof an earlier spelling "chrony." The charge of "government by croney" led David Brinkley to remark that a crony (or croney, or even chrony) is the friend of someone you don't like.

Among laudatory terms favored by the right wing on the international front are "the West" (only a geographical expression, but heavily invested with favorable overtones), and the more specific "Free World," which came into general use under Eisenhower, but is suspected of having been coined during World War II, to denote collectively those countries which had not succumbed to Nazi invasion.

Nations on our side are invariably referred to as "Allies," those on the other side as "satellites" or "puppets." "Puppet," dating back to 1550 as applied to persons, comes from French *poupée* and eventually from Latin *puppa*, "doll." A puppet state or regime is one which may be manipulated with strings. "Satellite" has a more interesting history. The Latin *satelles*, "retainer" or "attendant," is a word which Latin borrowed from Etruscan. Its first recorded use in English is in 1548, with the original Latin meaning; but in 1665 it got to be applied to a heavenly body whose movements are not independent, but predicated upon another and larger heavenly body. Today, a satellite state revolves around another state, and takes orders from it.

"Totalitarian" or "police state" may be indifferently applied to leftist or rightist regimes that show the features of not tolerating opposition, abolishing freedoms, and operating through the instrumentality of a well-organized secret police. "Slave economy" is likewise a strong, double-edged term for what might more mildly be styled a "controlled economy."

"Iron Curtain," first used in 1794 to describe a curtain that would prevent the spreading of fires in theaters, passed on to a variety of uses, notably one by H. G. Wells in 1904 to describe enforced privacy, before it entered international politics. The accusation that the West was trying to draw an "Iron Curtain" between itself and Russia was made in 1930 by *Literaturnaya Gazeta*. (*Cordon sanitaire* had been used previously in that sense, after the Bolshevik Revolution.) Joseph Goebbels, of Nazi propaganda fame, spoke of an iron curtain behind which millions would be butchered by the Reds if Germany laid down her arms. The classical "Iron Curtain" charge against the USSR was made, however, by Churchill in May of 1945. The term stuck, and gave rise to "Bamboo Curtain" when China joined the list of Communist states. "Purge," another loaded term, goes all the way back to 1648 and Cromwell, when Pride's Purge was used to get rid of Presbyterians and Royalists in Parliament. Today it is an all-purpose term, being used to describe even what goes on within traditional American parties. "Red Menace" is far more specific, and supplies the link between external and internal right-wing anti-Communist terminology.

On the domestic front, terms like "parlor pink," from which "pinko" is derived, go back to the days of Theodore Roosevelt; but as late as the 1920s a "parlor pink" was equated with a liberal or pacifist. Interestingly, the Oxford Dictionary does not have any political entry for "pink." "Peace front" began in 1933, but "Communist front" as a screen for Red activities is a later creation; the Oxford Dictionary does not offer it in this sense, but our later American dictionaries do. "Comsymp" for "Communist sympathizer" was the coinage of Robert Welch, founder of the John Birch Society, but did not meet with popular favor. "Fellow traveler," on the other hand, goes all the way back to the early days of Bolshevism, when Leon Trotsky used *poputchik* to describe sympathizers with Communism who were not party members. Another coinage whose origin is unknown is "anti-anti-Communist," describing people who defend Communism not directly, but by attacking those who oppose it. Three expressions attributed to the late Senator Joseph McCarthy are "soft on Communism," "twenty years of treason," and "security risk." "Party line," often used in an ironical sense by right-wing writers to describe activities that follow Communist directives, was used by Khrushchev in 1963, but originated with us at an earlier date, and not necessarily in connection with Communism, but rather by reason of the straight voting line on a ballot. Its coincidence with a telephone "party line" is a pure accident.

Two right-wing terms of opprobrium for opponents of the Vietnam war are "vietnik" and "peacenik." Here the *-nik* suffix, taken from Russian, became popular and productive at the time of Sputnik which, like *poputchik*, means "fellow traveler." (The root is *put'*, "road"; *s-* means "with"; *po-* has a variety of meanings, of which "in the manner of," "like," is the one that best applies; and both *-nik* and *-chik* are suffixes of agent.)

Three elegant creations are William Buckley's "ultra-liberal"; Edgar Mowrer's "instant democracy" to describe what our visionaries think can be achieved in such backward regions as Africa and Southeast Asia, and Ruth Nanda Anshen's "moral amnesia." The first was advanced in a syndicated column in which the Conservative leader called attention to the fact that whereas such prefixes as "extreme" and "ultra-" are often applied to conservatives, they never seem to be applied to liberals, save as a euphemism for "Communist." Why, he argued, should Senator Javits not be described as an "ultra-liberal Republican" rather than a "moderate Republican"? The objection is well taken, and we shall refer to the point again in our chapter on the Political Left.

The third coinage, offered by a distinguished philosopher, is presented not at all as a weasel word, but as an expression for which there is a crying need to describe a widespread phenomenon of our times. We have largely forgotten our moral sense, our sense of right and wrong. Relativism is rampant among us. Things, deeds, patterns of behavior are no longer regarded as intrinsically good or bad, but only in relation to existing circumstances. The moral code has become elastic. Worse yet, it has been conveniently forgotten. There is no absolute honesty, no absolute honor. There is only what you can get out of the world, the government, your fellow man. Not only does the end justify the means, but the end itself has become a vague, fluctuating entity, of which no one is quite sure.

What are we aiming at in our international policy? In our national and local politics? In our individual and family life? Just getting by, until death picks us up? The politician wants reelection at all costs; he straddles the fence and tries to please all groups, whether they be right or wrong. The statesman tells us we must coexist with evil, because the alternative is too horrible to contemplate. People of the Bertrand Russell persuasion tell us it is better to be red than dead. The businessman's sole concern is with profits. The laboring man's sole concern is higher wages and shorter hours. The young man out of college thinks only in terms of a soft, secure job; the young woman in terms of a soft, secure marriage. All want to get; no one wants to give.

The moral law is still the same. It cannot change. But if we cannot change it, we can conveniently forget it, put it out of our minds, pretend it isn't there. This is the basis and essence of the quality of Moral Amnesia, the disease that will sooner or later destroy us if a cure is not found for it.

CHAPTER 15

Thunder on the Left

As with the right, there is a left-wing vocabulary of traditional terms regarded with high approval. A few are such that they can safely be used by almost anybody, and invested with almost any desired meaning: "progressive," "forward-looking," "social justice." Even conservatives like to think of themselves as progressive and forward-looking, and social justice can range all the way from advocacy to resistance. A slight confusion attaches to "progressive" by reason of its use in connection with the income tax, but the context is usually clear. Even the recent use of "compassionate" and Senator Muskie's suggestion that we "trust" all people, including those who do not inspire much trust, can pass muster.

Real trouble begins with terms like "democratic" and "liberal," which have been invested with far too many meanings for their own good. "Democratic," by dictionary definition, means believing in government by the people or their freely elected representatives. One glance at the "democratic" republics of the Communist world suffices to warn us to use the term with extreme caution. There is a further complication by reason of the fact that in the United States "Democrat" and "Democratic," spelled with capitals, also refer to a political party, which started as Anti-Federalist, then became Republican, then prefixed "Democratic" to its name, and finally lost its second part, which was appropriated by the opposing side (Federalist, Whig, Republican). Dewey rather arbitrarily attempted to change the label of the Democratic Party, of which he formed no part, to "Democrat Party," but his innovation didn't take, and "Democrat" today is still used as a noun meaning a member of the party. "Democrat" was sneeringly applied by the Federalists to their opponents to imply that they were mobocrats, to which the others promptly replied by adopting the title and styling the Federalists "Aristocrats." Today, "democratic" is used, at least in this country, in the sense of popular consensus, with overtones of majority rule.

The case for "liberal" is far more complex. Here we pass from a connotation of freedom of the individual from excessive government restriction and supervision to the present-day conservative concept of "liberalism": laxity in morals, leftism, semi-socialism, and, above all, welfare statism, and unnecessary, unwanted government control—a definition which those who style themselves "liberals" firmly reject, even while they cheerfully accept and implement the implications. Dewey at one time claimed that the transmutation of the word was one of the wonders of our age. Others have claimed that "liberal" (using the term in the other sense of "generous") means "free and easy with other people's money"; and many taxpayers will agree.

Extending certain forms of freedom (by no means all; and, usually, the more controversial) through the instrumentality of government control seems to be the hallmark of modern American "liberalism" that has led its opponents to describe themselves as "libertarians." It is of interest, however, that whereas the Communist world has appropriated "democratic" and "republic" and turned them into mockeries, it has never attempted to distort "liberal" and "liberalism" in the same fashion.

Coming down to the immediate past, we find that the two best and most effective adaptations of the 1964 campaign were "mainstream" and "moderate." The former was used by the Rockefeller wing of the Republican Party to indicate what that wing wanted us to believe was the majority trend in that party. While its two component parts are very old in

English usage, they were not fused into a single unit, even with benefit of hyphen, until recent times, as evidenced by the fact that the 1932 Oxford Dictionary fails to record the compound. It appears, however, in the later American dictionaries, where it is defined, more or less, as "the prevailing current or direction." Objection, if any, would be only to its campaign use. On the face of it, judging from the manner in which the 1964 Republican National Convention voted, its application by the Rockefeller wing would seem unjustified. It was charged that Goldwater had won his top-heavy delegate majority by a series of stolen marches carried on well in advance of the convention while the opposition was presumably asleep. But the experience of the 1968 convention gave definite confirmation that the Republican mainstream is conservative, and that Rockefeller and his liberals were floating around in an eddy.

On the other hand, the application of the term "moderate" to describe the anti-conservative faction of the Republicans was such a triumph of semantic strategy that it may well have been thought up by the Democrats, Safire to the contrary. The only parallel that comes to mind is the earlier use of "temperance," in connection with "movement," to refer to rank Prohibitionism or teetotalism. "Temperance," starting with Latin *temperantia,* then going on into Old French and Middle English, had always meant "moderation," "self-restraint," "the avoidance of excesses, particularly in eating and drinking." The shift to the meaning of "total abstinence" came in 1834, when leaders of what earlier had been a true temperance movement, designed to do away with the evils of drunkenness, decided that "temperance" should mean "total abstention," not merely from the stronger spirituous liquors, but from alcohol in any amount and form, even beer and wine. It was with that meaning that American "temperance" organizations (the Women's Christian Temperance Union, the Methodist Board of Temperance, Prohibition and Public Morals, etc.) campaigned for the noble experiment of prohibition, which was to turn the United States into a land of scofflaws and bootleggers.

"Moderate" also goes back to Latin, where *moderatus* means "avoiding extremes," "using discretion and self-control," "tending toward the mean or average"; to use a modern paraphrase, "middle of the road." The word first appears in English in 1644, and finds its political application in 1753. It was applied to the Girondins in 1794, and the Girondins were indeed the most moderate among the French revolutionary parties that advocated a break with the feudal past, to the extent that they were lumped with the aristocrats and polished off on the guillotine by the followers of Marat, Danton, and Robespierre. The Oxford Dictionary informs us that around 1894 the word took a curious turn in British municipal elections, being opposed, of all things, to "progressive," particularly in the matter of do-good legislation calling for heavy expenditures. This would make the British "moderates" of the period approximately the equivalent of our ultra-conservatives.

Since "moderate," to an even greater extent than "temperance" and "mainstream," tends to create a highly favorable impression in a reasonable but uninformed mind, the pinning of such a label on a wing that included Rockefeller, Lodge, Javits, and Case, coupled with the opposite label of "extremist" fostered by Goldwater's own pronouncement on behalf of "extremism" (even though qualified by "in defense of liberty"), was probably enough to account for a couple of million votes when the showdown came. Even now, it is a favorite practice with left-wing editors and writers to describe as "extremist" anything and anybody that is conservative, and as "moderate" anything that is on the left, including numerous groups that agitate for a number of things, among them America's withdrawal from everywhere and leaving the world to the Russians and Chinese.

"Freedom" is a word to which hardly anyone will take

exception. It is supposed to have originated in Old English (*freodom*), but its earliest examples do not antedate the Middle English period. Its first element is derived from an Indo-European root which, interestingly, also bears the connotations of "love" and "friendship." The semantic implication would seem to be that true love and true friendship cannot be imposed, but must arise freely and spontaneously. At any rate, the word is generally defined as "the quality of being free or uncoerced; self-determination; exemption or liberation from slavery, imprisonment, restraint, or the arbitrary, tyrannical power of another."

The "Four Freedoms" is a phrase which, naturally enough, does not appear in the Oxford Dictionary or the older Webster. It is defined in the 1961 Webster as "the four basic freedoms identified by Franklin Delano Roosevelt as freedom of speech and expression, freedom of worship, freedom from want and freedom from fear."

To the extent that we accept the definition of "freedom" given above, one can hardly quarrel with the first two of Roosevelt's basic freedoms, though one could easily add a list of others equally basic—for example, the freedom to leave if one is dissatisfied where he is; the freedom to gather and enjoy the fruits of one's own labor; the freedom to associate with whom one pleases, at least in private activities.

The last two of Roosevelt's freedoms, by the same token, are not freedoms at all. At best, they might be described as desirable social goals, destined by their very nature to remain forever unattained and unattainable, but which one may strive for as he strives after perfection.

The only true freedom from want (and we may be wrong even on this point) is that which one achieves in the grave. The dead body, to the best of our material knowledge, wants nothing more, once it is laid to rest. It is the want of something that is at the root of all human activity, whether industrial, commercial, political, religious, cultural, sexual, or what have you. Freedom from want would mean the death of ambition, longing, aspiration, desire, hope. It would be the worst gift that one man could confer upon another, or society upon the individual.

Semantically and socially, "freedom from want" is a dangerous hoax. It is only through want, through a sense of lacking something desirable, that mankind can achieve higher goals. Take away from a living organism (vegetable, animal, or human) its wants, and you have conversion from the organic to the inorganic, from the living organism to the lifeless object.

"Freedom from fear" is another semantic and social hoax. Fear is inherent in all living things. We may be temporarily freed from certain specific fears, we may be granted a sense of partial security in some respects, but fear remains—the overlying fear of cessation. The man without fear is not brave, he is rash, a menace to himself and others. If Roosevelt had in mind fear of political, religious, or racial persecution, he should have said so. (Actually, his partial clarification dealt more with fear of international wars than anything else.)

"Freedom from" is a negative, not a positive freedom. Freedom must be active, dynamic, an exercise of one's faculties and prerogatives, not a supine acceptance of some form of security. It must be the freedom to do something, a "freedom of," or a "freedom to." The time has come to replace false freedoms with real ones.

Two other words favored by left-wingers of the do-good variety are "underprivileged" and "disadvantaged."

"Privilege" comes from Latin *priva lex*, "private law," a law specifically on behalf of or against a private individual. By the time "privilege" reaches Middle English, it already means "a special right or immunity, a personal right as opposed to the common right; a prerogative."

"Underprivileged" gives us pretty much the same picture on the home front that "underdeveloped" carries in international relations. Senator La Follette is described as having used it, but not necessarily as having coined it. The word had apparently not penetrated Britain at the time of the compilation of the 1932 Oxford Dictionary, nor does it come into the 1950 Addenda. The Random House Dictionary speaks of "the normal privileges and rights of society, denied because of low economic and social status." The 1961 Webster defines it as "being debarred from an average standard of living; being deprived, through social or economic oppression, of the fundamental rights theoretically belonging to all members of a civilized society." Thus we are made to feel that it is all our fault. People are not poor because they are shiftless and unwilling to better themselves; they are poor because they are oppressed, debarred, deprived, held down. There is a whole world of semantic overtones in that one little word "underprivileged."

Those of us who rose out of a poorer into a more affluent state through our own initiative and hard work were seldom conscious of being "underprivileged" in the sense described above. We knew the remedy was in our own hands, since we lived in a basically free society. "Underprivileged" is a word that might well be reserved for those inhabitants of Communist paradises (and they are the overwhelming majority) who for one reason or another have found it impossible to join the local Communist Party. We who are free to come and go, to move from one state to another, and even out of the country if we so choose, to relinquish and seek employment as we see fit, can describe ourselves as millionaires, rich, well-to-do, poor, even desperately poor. We have no right to describe ourselves as over- or underprivileged. No man of wealth or standing can commit murder with impunity, as do the Communist hierarchies. Due process of law is there for everyone. So is economic opportunity, if one cares to avail himself of it. There is no "private law" here.

"Disadvantaged" seems a later euphemism, and still does not appear in the Oxford Dictionary, though "disadvantage," from Middle English, and "disadvantageous" are given. The

Old French form from which the Middle English is derived goes back to a horripilating Vulgar Latin compound *de-ex-ab-ante-aticum*, "away-from-before-state"; in other words, you are away from being in the front ranks of wealth and privilege. The Random House Dictionary speaks of lacking the usual advantages, such as a good home and friends, but Webster's Third, more social-minded, adds deprivation of medical and educational facilities, and even civil rights, before referring you to the synonym "underprivileged." A 1963 news item in our possession defines the disadvantaged as those with an annual income of less than $2000 (it has gone up to $3000 now, by reason of inflation), and mentions American Indians, Appalachian whites, and Mexican migrant workers as typical. A 1965 Jules Feiffer cartoon shows the progression from "poor" to "needy" to "deprived" to "underprivileged" to "disadvantaged," with the comic strip character adding that while he still doesn't have a dime, he has acquired a fine vocabulary.

One final item of left-wing approval is in connection with that universal panacea for all the social ills that affect us, taxation, particularly of the progressive income variety. In an editorial of an otherwise excellent New Jersey daily (the *Newark Star-Ledger*), advocacy of a state income tax is supported by a battery of flowery expressions of which we may report a few fragments, *ut ab uno discas omnes:* "fiscal realism"; "critically-needed funds for educational purposes"; "new tax posture"; "a broader, viable tax structure, designed to nurture the state's growth and meet growing responsibilities in education, mass transit and expanded aid to municipalities"; "fiscal dynamism"; "generating new revenues"; "the state's taxing spectrum"; "criteria of equity"; "march into the future with boldness of purpose and the fiscal assurance that New Jersey can do the things that must be done." This monumental sample of left-wing weaselry in connection with left-wing tax-and-spendomania deserves to be immortalized for posterity. The only wonder is that it failed to convince New Jersey voters.

If the left-wing vocabulary of approval is large, that of disapproval is even larger. General terms range from the ancient "Tory," whose early history we traced in our opening chapter, and which is occasionally applied to conservatives today; and "reactionary," which goes back to the French Revolution, to the disparaging "horse-and-buggy" coined by Roosevelt in 1934 and equated by Webster's Third to "hopelessly outdated," and the "little old ladies in tennis shoes," scornfully applied to feminine supporters of Goldwater in the 1964 campaign.

But there are other choice epithets: "hidebound" (this, in its literal meaning, goes back to 1559 and, as applied to bigots, to 1603); "mossback" (from Southern draft dodgers in Civil War days, who took to the swamps); "anti-social" (starting in 1797 in the sense of "timid," "shy," then going on to "hostile," and achieving in 1849 the meaning of "opposed to the social order"). Republicans are described as "rock-ribbed" (from Bryant's *Thanatopsis;* but this is rather flattering); "rank" (in the sense of "rancid"); and "black." This last is claimed to go back to pre-Civil War days, when it was bestowed in 1854 upon Republicans because of their sympathies with black slaves; but we wonder whether some of the imagery may not have rubbed off from the earlier "Black Protestant," used in Ireland. "Old Guard" was first applied to Republican conservatives in 1844, but it goes back to those soldiers of Napoleon who, under Cambronne, refused to surrender at Waterloo. Two fairly recent creations to describe the Far Right are "Neanderthal Wing," said to have originated with Judge Rosenman, FDR's advisor, and "Dinosaur Wing," attributed to Adlai Stevenson. "China Lobby," of 1946, is used to describe those Americans who think we would have done better to support Chiang Kai-Shek rather than to rely on the "agrarian reformism" of Mao Tse-tung.

Economic terms of left-wing opprobrium include "Special (or "Vested") Interests" (but "vested interests" originated in Britain with Macaulay in 1857), and "Special Privilege," coined by La Follette; "Malefactors of Great Wealth," circulated by Theodore Roosevelt in 1907, and both "economic royalists" and "plutocrats," devised by his kinsman FDR. "Monopoly" is a word frequently used in the course of trust-busting activities. On the class front, we have the classic "Babbitt" (with its derivative "Babbitry"), coined by Sinclair Lewis in 1923 to typify the materialistic American businessman (now replaced by the "suburbanite" or "Upper Slobovian"); as well as the elegant British "U" (short for "upper class," and flanked by its opposite, "non-U"; but this coinage has become almost entirely restricted to language features). "Merchants of Death," to describe armaments manufacturers who profit from wars and the rumors of wars, used as the title of a book in the 1920s, is far-reaching in its modern implications, and cannot be altogether dismissed as mere propaganda. Neither can the "Oil Barons" of Texas. Nor the "military-industrial complex" first mentioned by Eisenhower in his 1961 farewell address, in which he warned us of its dangers.

There is a much stronger left-wing terminology, which is used to belabor the really Far Right. Some of it has racial overtones, and will be discussed in an appropriate chapter ("hatemonger," "apostle of hate," "racist," etc.). Here belong also "genocide," invented by Raphael Lemkin in 1944, and the ambiguous "anti-Semitism" and "anti-Semitic," used as a euphemism for "anti-Jewish"; the absurdity of this usage was demonstrated when the Arab nations, themselves fully Semitic as to origin and language, were accused of preaching and practicing "anti-Semitism."

Terms with regional overtones are "redneck" and "cracker," applied to ignorant Southern whites who are rightly or wrongly accused of being both anti-Negro and anti-progress.

The first goes back to 1830, the second has been in circulation since 1767. No satisfactory semantic explanation appears for the first, while the Oxford Dictionary, with a question mark, suggests "whipcracker" as the source of the second (but poor Southern whites were not, as a rule, slaveowners, and consequently would not be cracking whips over the blacks, save in the rare capacity of overseers). Geographically, "redneck" seems to be in more general use in Alabama, Mississippi, and Louisiana, while "cracker" flourishes in Georgia and Florida. There is also an unsubstantiated claim that "redneck" is applied to Catholics in West Virginia. Three additional, highly picturesque terms used in the 1968 campaign by Governor Wallace to describe parts of his own following are "woolhat" (described in Webster's Third as a small Georgia farmer); "peckerwood" (a Southern poor white); and "pea picker." One imaginative and fairly recent term coined by Senator Morse is "Nixocrat," defined as a "Dixiecrat with a Yankee accent."

"Patrioteer," a sneering term for an American jingoist, has gone out of fashion (it appears in Webster's Third, but not in the more recent Random House Dictionary). Senator Fulbright's "Arrogance of Power" is meant to be an indictment of the more aggressive features of American foreign policy, with Soviet and Chinese aggressiveness conveniently forgotten.

There are words from the days of Hitler and Mussolini that are resurrected on occasion and applied to the domestic scene: "Brown Shirt," "Black Shirt," "Storm Trooper," "Fascist," "fascistic," "neo-Fascist." "Lunatic fringe," coined by Theodore Roosevelt in 1913 to describe extreme leftists, was curiously brought back to life with reversed meaning by Franklin Roosevelt in 1944. The "lunatic fringe" is described in certain writings as being to the right of the Dinosaur Wing of the rightists. "John Birch Society" may be dispassionately discussed, both as a term and an institution, but "John Bircher" is definitely a left-wing epithet, coined in 1953. "Birchism" and "Birchite" came later, but are less frequently used, since they appear in Webster's Third but not in the Random House Dictionary.

Numerous vocabulary items go back to the days of Senator Joseph McCarthy. "McCarthyism" itself, coined by Herbert Block ("Herblock") in 1950 as a term of general revilement, was interestingly used against Johnson supporters by another McCarthy, Eugene, in the 1968 campaign, when aspersions were cast upon his patriotism by Administration henchmen. Webster's Third, following leftist usage, equates McCarthyism with the Know-Nothingism of an earlier day, and in its definition speaks of "indiscriminate, unsubstantiated charges." Among terms that came into vogue during the McCarthy era are "Red-baiting," "witch-hunting" (this refers to the witch trials in Salem in the seventeenth century, featuring persecution of innocent people based on superstitious fear and insufficient evidence), and "book-burning," which Safire reminds us not only came into vogue in Hitler's Germany in 1933, but was known even in the China of the third century B.C.

A few other left-wing favorites are more subtle, and bear more searching scrutiny.

In addition to Buckley's "ultra-," previously described, there is another vogue term among the leftists, "extreme right." "Extreme," going back to the Latin original, is broadly defined by Webster's Third in a political sense as "going to great or exaggerated lengths, uncompromising, radical, fanatical." Its first recorded appearance in English is in 1460. The Oxford does not shed light upon its first recorded use in politics, but does set 1588 as the initial date for "something carried to excess, as 'an extreme measure.' " "Right," an old Anglo-Saxon word etymologized elsewhere in this work, acquired a political connotation only in 1787, and then with reference to continental European political chambers. The 1961 Webster defines it politically as "the part of a legislative assembly located to the right of the presiding officer, and usually occupied, in European and other countries, by members professing a more conservative or rightist position on political issues than other members," and gives as an example "the right is occupied by a Neo-Fascist group"; this does not appear as a quote, and we may assume that it is the editors' own creation. The 1884 Webster does not even mention "right" in a political sense. The use of "extreme right" and "extreme left" in languages other than English is widespread and of long standing.

It would appear that the division of political parties into right and left represents a tradition that is alien to Anglo-Saxon institutions, and this is borne out by the location of the opposition benches in the British Parliament. Be this as it may, there can be no real objection, in these days of heated political and economic controversy, to the existence and use of terms such as "extreme right" and "extreme left."

The only objection is to their application. When "extreme right" is used, on the one hand, to describe any sort of conservative movement, even of the most peaceable and law-abiding variety, as exemplified below, while on the other hand "extreme right" is equated, at least by implication, with Neo-Fascism, as in Webster's Third, then we have the famous case in logic of two things that are equal to a third thing being equal to each other.

Let us take as an example this editorial fragment, appearing in the *Columbia Daily Spectator* for Wednesday, March 7, 1962: "At Madison Square Garden, the Young Americans for Freedom, an extreme right wing group, will meet to present awards and hear speakers . . . [such as Senator Barry Goldwater]. A few blocks away, at the St. Nicholas Arena, liberal students will gather to express their opposition to the YAF program. . . ." No mention is made in the editorial that among the prime sponsors of the St. Nicholas Arena program were the Americans for Democratic Action, who could be considered as much of an extreme left group as the YAF are extreme right. Actually, both meetings took place in very orderly fashion, and there was no clash or violence of any kind. We just wonder why the YAF should be labeled "an extreme right wing group," with all the Neo-Fascist connotations involved. To our knowledge, they have never indulged in activities that could be even remotely described as questionable or violent, though they agitate, as is their right as American citizens, for various changes in policy, both foreign and domestic.

Does this "extreme right" business not constitute name-calling? Is is not in the nature of a smear? Does it not tend to restrict the rights of American citizens to speak freely on their government's policies? Ought not the label "extreme right," insofar as it has to be used, to be reserved for avowedly Hitlerian and Nazi groups, and not be indiscriminately applied to organizations that merely advocate more conservative policies both at home and abroad, coupled with freedom of expression for such foreign leaders as Tshombe who happen to favor the West rather than the Soviets in the cold war?

Another modern combination is "character assassination." We seek it in vain in the older Webster, the Oxford Dictionary, and the modern Random House Dictionary. The Oxford Dictionary informs us that "assassination" first appeared in English in 1605. ("Assassin," the base word, goes back to the *Hashisheen*, or hashish eaters, a fanatical Moslem set that opposed the Crusaders in the Holy Land by methods that today would be described as guerrilla warfare or *résistance*.) The 1961 Webster's Third defines the combination as "the slandering of another person (as a public figure) with the intention of destroying public trust in him"—a picturesque figure of speech, and one which, by its very nature, would have numerous applications in all sorts of fields, including the academic. The only objection is to its overuse and misuse in the political sphere. In some instances, any reference to a person's past activities or associations, true or false, is described as "character assassination."

There is no doubt that a good deal of this goes on. Nor is there any doubt that when the slander is real slander (consisting of untruths) the process is reprehensible. On the other hand, people occupying or seeking positions of public trust ought to be prepared to face their own past, which is often an indication of the future course they may be expected to pursue. To label a truthful *exposé* "character assassination" is, to say the least, an exaggeration. It may also be pointed out that the smearing process is by no means a monopoly of the right wing, extreme or otherwise. Let us therefore put "character assassination" in its proper perspective, and then go on using it.

"Guilt by association" is another interesting word-combination favored by leftists. It is defined, only in the 1961 Webster, as "moral guilt or unfitness presumed to exist on the basis of one's known associations." The entry then goes on to explain in parentheses that "the doctrine of guilt by association has on occasion been used to brand as currently disloyal persons who at some past time had been members of an organization not known to be or considered subversive at the time they were members."

It is, of course, anyone's prerogative, not merely that of members of the feminine sex, to change one's mind, and even reverse one's original stand. The codicil appearing in the Webster definition may also have historical justification. At the same time, guilt by association is a practice that far antedates present political controversies. Practically every language, ancient or modern, has the equivalent of "Birds of a feather flock together." (Some are even more pointed; the Italian proverb, for instance, says: "Tell me whom you go with, and I'll tell you who you are.") Man is generally known by the company he keeps, at least where he has the choice.

It is interesting in connection with the element of choice that anti-Nazi and anti-Fascist proceedings were often instituted against people who claimed and often could prove that they had been forced to join those parties under penalty of losing their jobs and means of livelihood. This disclaimer is generally not available in a land such as ours, where people are altogether free to select both their personal friends and the groups to which they choose to belong. Hence "guilt by association" is not quite so reprehensible a practice as it might appear at first glance. If a man is forever in the company of known subversives, and holds or has held membership in numerous groups of a subversive nature, there may be some legitimate doubt as to whether he should be encouraged to seek or hold public office in a country devoted to principles and institutions which those same subversive groups seek to destroy.

This brings us down to that well-known bugaboo of the liberal mind known as the "loyalty oath." (There is no point to defining or giving the history of Anglo-Saxon *oath*, while *loyalty*, from Old French, is defined as "fidelity, allegiance, fealty.") The 1961 Webster, the only work that deals with the combination, defines the loyalty oath as "a usually mandatory oath affirming the loyalty of its taker (as to a sovereign, government, or party principle), an oath often required of public employees or applicants for public employment in the U.S., typically affirming that the signer upholds the U.S. or state constitution and is not knowingly a member of any of a number of organizations held to be subversive." This appears to be quite accurate, and the term "loyalty oath" can be accepted to cover the situation. But in certain quarters there is an aura of opprobrium attached to the expression. "Loyalty oath" becomes a synonym for a violation of both conscience and constitutional rights.

Yet it should be recognized that this oath is nowhere administered indiscriminately. The man who does not believe in the federal or state constitution is not compelled to give up his beliefs. It is only the seeker after public office or employment of whom the oath is required. Since American constitutions, both federal and state, contain liberal provision for their own orderly change (we could turn ourselves into a totalitarian state of the Fascist or Communist type if we were so minded, by a thoroughly constitutional process of amendment), it would seem as though the only ones who could object to the oath would be those who advocate change by violence. It would seem a little dangerous for the rest of us to have such people in positions of public trust.

Other arguments against the loyalty oath of the American type do not hold much water. To say that it singles out some individuals as being the objects of suspicion is answered by the obvious fact that they single themselves out by applying or running for public posts, and that there is no true element of suspicion attached. If there were, the President of the United States, the Cabinet officers, the justices of the Supreme Court and other courts, members of the armed forces, and all high-ranking government officials should feel themselves to be the objects of undeserved suspicion, for they all take an oath of office which is to all intents and purposes a loyalty oath. The same would apply to foreigners seeking naturalization. The oath rather enhances the dignity of the one who takes it, since it singles him out as being specifically worthy of a post of national or public trust. Why feel humiliated? Ought we not rather to feel proud, so long as the oath is to a nation and a constitution, and not to an individual or party? Ought we not to class the loyalty oath with the oath of allegiance of the prospective citizen, the pledge to the flag of the schoolboy, and the presidential oath of office?

There is also an answer to the objection that the crypto-Communist will take the oath with the full intention of breaking it, so what is the use of administering it to him? If he takes the oath and breaks it, he may be prosecuted for perjury. If he doesn't take it, and is later proved to be a

Communist, no prosecution is possible, because our enlightened liberalism grants people the right to join any group
they please. As is right and proper? Perhaps. But members
of groups vowed to overthrow our institutions by violence
should not be in posts of public trust, Supreme Court decisions to the contrary.

CHAPTER 16

Common Communese

The existence of an international vocabulary of Communism has long been recognized, and choice segments have appeared in numerous newspaper and magazine articles. One writer, Roy Colby, has even produced a complete book on the subject. We are all aware of the feeling of profound disgust, as well as aversion, that fills us when we read a communiqué from North Korea, North Vietnam, or Red China, or even a Soviet-produced article or pronouncement, filled with unbelievably florid, fulsome phrases or with bitter invective, according to the subject matter. "How can these people be so naive as to think anybody will take this sort of talk seriously?" we wonder. "What distorted type of mind can lie behind this misuse of ordinary language?"

What we must recall is that the vocabulary of Communism has been evolved over more than a century; that it has many ramifications, depending on the use for which it is designed; that some of its roots go back to other, highly legitimate fields, such as labor relations, economics, even religion; and that while it may strike the more sophisticated among us as laughable, it is swallowed, bait, hook and sinker, by many (but by no means all) of the devotees of Communism. Communism has been described as a form of religion, albeit a godless one, with its own ritual liturgy, litany of saints, and infernal legions. Considering its lengthy history, its variety of approaches, the boundless gullibility of many (again, by no means all) of its adepts, it is no wonder that an entire volume can be filled with its highly specialized terminology.

But that terminology is very much stratified. There are terms of ordinary administration, like Soviet Russia's "Presidium," "Cominform," and "Comintern," "New Economic Policy," "Ogpu," and "N.K.V.D." There is the language of ordinary propaganda, designed for both internal and foreign consumption. There is the mysterious Aesopian jargon, by which the Communist hierarchies manage to communicate with and direct their underlings abroad without seeming to. There is a vocabulary of obloquy reserved for the capitalistic world, and another for internecine use among the various Communist powers—terms of accusation which the Communist factions hurl at one another whenever they disagree as to the methods (never the ultimate purpose) of their relentless campaign to enslave the world. Only a sampling of each can be offered here.

The old, traditional vocabulary of Communism from the days of Marx and Engels relied heavily upon the nascent labor movement. There were such terms as laboring-class "solidarity," "workers" (this appears in "Workers of the world, unite!"), but the later tendency is to substitute "toilers," which carries heavier overtones of hard, physical, manual labor; more recently, we have had "simple toilers" and "broad masses," those members of the laboring classes who are not in the Party, but take their orders from the hierarchy. There is the "class struggle" and the "class enemy," the "dictatorship of the proletariat," described as the first step in organizing a Communist society. ("Proletariat" goes back to Latin *proles*, "offspring"; a "proletarian" in early Roman society was a man who had no wealth, and could serve the state only with his offspring. "Class struggle," or "class war," or "class conflict" arose as expressions in the 1920s, but "class" in the social sense first appears in 1772.)

Among the more elegant creations of the Marxist Founding Fathers was "materialism"; this can be "dialectical," "historical," or "economic"; the basic idea is that there is no spirit; all is infinite matter; history evolves inexorably, from a feudal to a bourgeois to a single-class structure; in the Marxist view, man's actions are motivated solely by economic causes.

This early segment of the Communist vocabulary has at least the merit of being frank and unmistakable. When it is used, we know who is using it and what is being driven at.

Trouble starts when the Communists begin to use in a special sense terms that are in the common vocabulary, particularly those in frequent use by leftists who are not Communists. At one time, a pamphlet prepared by the Army and entitled *How to Spot a Red* drew fire from the Civil Liberties Union and other "liberal" organizations because it listed, among supposedly significant clues, the frequent use of such words as "progressive," "peace," "military budget," "violation of civil rights," "racial and religious discrimination," "labor union legislation," even "fluoridation of the water supply," all terms which might be used by anybody. There were slightly more meaningful terms, such as "vanguard," "chauvinism," "demagogy," "reactionary," "exploitation," but these are still in the twilight zone. More significant still were words of the type of "book-burning," "witchhunting," "colonialism," "McCarthyism," "police brutality," "anti-subversive legislation," all of which are characteristic of the left wing, but not at all necessarily of Communists. Then came some dead giveaways like "dialectical materialism" and "ruling classes." There is no question that a better selection could have been made.

But neither is there question that many of the above innocent-sounding terms, and lots of others besides, are used in the Aesopian language with a meaning that is known only to the initiate, and will be taken at face dictionary value by everyone else unless he is forewarned. "Peace," for instance, in the Communist view means cessation of all opposition to Communism and the acceptance of a Communist world. The

implications of "peace-loving" then become crystal-clear
"Unity" means universal submission to Communist discipline
and rule. "Voluntary" implies consent brought about through
various forms of pressure, including brainwashing and torture
"War" is resistance to Communism (a war launched by the
Communists is invariably styled "liberation" or "heroic resistance to imperialistic aggression"). "Aggression" is armed
conflict against the Reds, even of a purely defensive nature
(The South Koreans were guilty of "aggression" when they
resisted the North Korean invasion, and the South Vietnamese
are similarly guilty when they battle the Vietcong.) "People'
does not mean all human beings, but only those accepted
as legal entities under Communism. The others ("party
enemies") may at the most be dignified by the term "masses.'
"Non-interference" means not obstructing Communist aims
or actions. "Scientific" means in accord with Communist
mysticism, and "tolerance" means acceptance by non-Com-
munists of Communist teachings.

In Communist parlance, "democratic" means Communistic
(see "Democratic People's Republics"). "Independent" means
subservient to Moscow. A "free election" is a thoroughly
rigged, one-slate affair. Even "neutrality" is defined in Maxim
Litvinoff's book on USSR foreign policy in these terms: "In
the contemporary imperial system, a treaty of neutrality is
nothing but one of the elements in the preparation for war."
Roy Colby offers a set of translations from the Communese
of the Hanoi government into standard English, rendering
each term by its true meaning. A partial list follows:

When a Communist says:	*He means:*
patriotic	pro-Communist
compatriot	fellow-Communist
heroic acts	treasonable crimes
monstrous crimes	U.S. military successes
provocations	defensive steps

uild a free and happy life	undergo Communist regimentation
nankind	international Communism
iberate	conquer
iberated	brought under Communist control
rogressive	following the Communist party line
emocratic regime	Communist colonialism
andlords	landowners
and reform	confiscation
ressgang mercenaries	U.S. troops

In addition to these true weasel words, there are other lements of the Communist vocabulary that don't fool anyone oo much. A "historic crime" is anything you may have done r said against Communism at any time in your life, for vhich you will be duly punished if the Reds ever take over. When they speak of "liquidating" their opponents, most of s realize that the true meaning is exterminating them. This ften takes place after a "people's trial," the sort of summary arce carried on by Castro in Cuba after he took over from bloody" Batista. Communist movements and societies are lescribed as "monolithic" (built out of a single rock) and peace-loving," but we have seen the rock being cleft asunder y dissension and the love of peace manifested by such overnments as those of Pyong Yang, Hanoi, Peking, and Moscow. "National Liberation Fronts" are generally known or what they are: Red gangster groups.

The "War of National Liberation" is something that on ure dictionary grounds could well be applied to the uprising f Budapest's Freedom Fighters and the ill-fated exploit of he Cuban exiles at the Bay of Pigs as well as to the Vietamese and Algerian revolts against the French colonial egime. But in the Aesopian language of the Communists and ellow-travelers, it is applied also to such adventures as that of Che Guevara in Bolivia, where a dozen or so foreign agitators try to stir up an indifferent local population into revolt. We are left in doubt as to whether it is applicable to Biafra's separatism from Nigeria, the Angolan uprisings of a few years ago, or Tshombe's attempt to separate Katanga from the Congo. It all depends on which side of the fence you're on. The expression receives no recognition in our dictionaries; but the Random House Dictionary does give "National Liberation Front," which is equated to the Vietcong.

There are many other terms that are regarded with favor by the Reds, both within the movement and flanking it. Among the latter is the good old *Front Populaire*, or "Popular Front" of Léon Blum's prewar France, which preceded the collapse of what was rated as the best army in the world, before the onset of the Nazis to whom the Communists were then allied. This term first arose in Spain (*Frente Popular*) in the early 1930s, to denote a coalition of left-wing parties, dominated by the Communists, for the ostensible common purpose of opposing Fascism, but with the ultimate aim, known only to the Communists, of installing a Communist regime once the Fascists were cleared away. Then there are the "Lincoln" and "Jefferson Brigades" that fought on the so-called Loyalist side in the Spanish Civil War, composed of young idealists who did not realize that they were giving their lives for the Communist conspiracy; or the "Better Red than dead" slogan of Bertrand Russell, occasionally voiced today by people who have no idea what they would be letting themselves in for. (This has a precursor in "Peace at Any Price," first coined by the poet Lamartine in 1848, and later used by numerous appeasers on the most disparate occasions.)

Among themselves, the Communists love to speak of "fraternal cooperation" among the Communist countries (the sort of thing exemplified in the Russian invasions of Hungary and Czechoslovakia). A "planned Socialist economy" is a phrase often used to betoken the fully controlled system of

Communism, and "full employment" is the euphemism that covers up forced labor. There is even "creative Marxism," an expression coined by Khrushchev to indicate that when Marxist theory breaks down in the face of practical economics, it may be bypassed or even ignored.

One well-known term in use among Communists is "comrade." This has been in common Communist use since 1884, but it entered English in 1591, going back to medieval Spanish *camarada*, "roommate," "one who shares a room with you." To get away from the obvious implications of the term, Ulbricht's East German Communists have put into circulation an equivalent term not yet tarred with the Red brush, "colleague," in English use since 1534. Its etymology is from Latin words meaning "with" and "choose," "one who is chosen at the same time you are." I think there may be reason to surmise that the abbreviated "Commie" may represent a blend of "Communist" and "comrade."

Communist China has in recent times offered us a special term, "Cultural Revolution," which seems to have been coined as late as 1965. It is a translation of Chairman Mao's wen^2-hwa^1 ge^2-$ming^1$, and the translated term is so recent that it finds its way into none of our major dictionaries. (Webster's Third gives us "cultural evolution," the Random House Dictionary "cultural lag," but these are entirely different things.) The literal translation of the four Chinese characters is "refined-influence (or change) remove-mandate"; transformation by good influence, but with a removal of the mandate to rule. "Cultural revolution" would seem to refer to the anthropological rather than the traditional meaning of "culture" (the sum total of a social group's customs, ways, and habits of thought). In practice, the cultural revolution as carried out by Mao's Red Guards involves the obliteration of China's ancient culture and its replacement by the drab contents of the Chairman's little red book, with the concomitant destruction of monuments, works of literature and philosophy, and anything else that might remind the

Chinese that they were once a highly civilized race. If we replace the anthropological definition of "culture" with the older one that makes "culture" synonymous with "civilization," then "culturicide" might be a better rendering of the concept, if not of the words.

The Communist vocabulary of obloquy against the capitalistic world has already been exemplified. The favorite triad consists of "imperialistic," "capitalistic," and "colonialistic," which are regularly used to describe any Western, particularly American, institutions or activities, in complete oblivion of the fact that there are no greater or more objectionable imperialisms and colonialisms than those of the USSR and Red China. (For the former, consider the cases of Poland, Hungary, Czechoslovakia, Rumania, Bulgaria, held by the Soviet Union as subject and satellite states, plus Lithuania, Latvia, Estonia, parts of Finland and Germany, forcibly annexed during and after World War II, plus the Ukraine, the Armenian and Georgian regions, and all of Siberia and Russian Turkestan, whose colonization goes back to the days of the Czars; for the latter, we can think of Manchuria, Mongolia, Tibet, and the Chinese sphere of influence over North Korea and North Vietnam, which was almost extended to Indonesia, plus the aggression perpetrated against India.) One rather ingenious linguistic creation that unfortunately did not take hold was Sukarno's "Necolim" (for Neo-Colonialism-Imperialism), which came out shortly before he was shorn of most of his power. It is well for these mouth-filling phrases of anti-Americans to be condensed into briefer and more readily usable forms.

"Bourgeois," to describe the great middle-class enemy, goes back to the days of Marx in its Communist acceptance, but entered English from French in 1564 in the sense of "burgher"; it then passed on in 1674 to "member of the middle or merchant class"; finally it acquired the sense of "materialistic capitalist," scorned not only by the Communists, but also by those who prize spiritual and intellectual values. In this sense, it is almost synonymous with "Babbitt." Used as an adjective, it is sometimes combined with certain nouns, to express certain concepts. "Bourgeois reformism," for instance, means any desirable reforms that are carried on by capitalist regimes outside of and without the blessing of the Communists; however worthy, bourgeois reformism is something to be ridiculed and opposed at all costs, because only Communist reforms lead to true happiness for the masses. "Bourgeois sentimentality" is the term used to define any tolerance of Western ideas by Communists or Communist states; the Czechs were heavy sinners in this respect, and had to be shown their error. "Bourgeois morality" has to do with the old, traditional virtues and views of the Christian world, and was at first thrown into the ashcan by the Bolsheviks; but it now shows distressing signs of resurgence in the Soviet Union, where free love, pornography, and even miniskirts are frowned upon.

Since it is only capitalistic countries, by definition, that wage "war," the terms "chauvinist," "warmongers," "jingoists," "aggressors," "interventionists," "hooligans," even "cannibals" are properly applied only to them. Some of these terms have interesting histories. "Chauvinism," for instance, a term that arose in 1870, is based on a legendary veteran of Napoleon's armies, Nicolas Chauvin ("Chauvin" means "warm wine") who was satirized in a comedy for his excessive patriotism. "Jingoist" comes from the expression "by jingo," used since 1670 as a conjurer's invocation, but brought into nationalistic use in 1876–1878, at a time when trouble was brewing between Britain and Russia, and a popular song, in which "by jingo" appeared, became symbolical of overheated British feelings. "Hooligan" and "hooliganism" arose in 1898, and "Hooligan" is said to have been the name of a very unruly Irish family in Southwark. The Random House Dictionary gives it as the equivalent of "rowdy," and speculates that it may be a variant of the more common Irish family name

Houlihan, being borne out in this by the regular shift of *h* in Western names to *g* in Cyrillic transcriptions; while Webster's Third, following the Russian interpretation, defines a "hooligan" as the representative of special interests who overrides the rights of others, civil or otherwise. Against the derivation from Houlihan is the fact that an American comic strip once featured a tramp character named "Happy Hooligan," antedating the Bolshevik Revolution. In this country the term has become somewhat obsolete.

Capitalistic countries are also guilty of sponsoring "mad armament races" and of working against Communist interests and on behalf of "American monopolies" through their "myrmidons." These were the Thessalian followers of Achilles who acted as his personal army in the Trojan War. The term came into use in English in 1649 with the meaning of "ruffians," "hirelings," "unscrupulous retainers who carry out their leader's will without question and at any cost." "Yankee go home" is probably of Russian Communist origin, and arose at the end of World War II, particularly in occupied Berlin. But the Chinese Communists have also discovered that we are only "paper tigers." This expression seems to have been coined by Mao in 1946, with the imagery that something that is only painted on paper cannot be dangerous or do any real harm. Even the atom bomb is a paper tiger, in the Chairman's conception.

One interesting term is "manipulated democracy," the situation under which the capitalist power structure allegedly controls all political parties and presents the voters with meaningless choices between hand-picked candidates. (We have been known to use "Tweedledum and Tweedledee" in this sense.) There is some justification for this view, as evidenced by many of our nominating conventions; but our choice is still broader than that offered under Communism.

"Cosmopolitanism" is the charge leveled by Communists against Jews, whose internationalism is of a different brand from that advocated by Moscow. At any rate, it supplies a convenient excuse both for persecuting the Jews in the USSR and for opposing Israel.

Since the loudly trumpeted "monolithic unity" of the Communist world is not all that it is cracked up to be, and rifts periodically appear both in the Communist hierarchies and among the Communist nations, there is a vocabulary of disapproval that is meant for purely internal consumption, and is never applied to the non-Communist world. But before we reach it, there is a series of words of scorn that may be described as ambivalent; that is, they may be equally applied to the anti-Communists of the capitalist countries and to dissident elements within the Communist structure. "Spies," "wreckers," "fiends," "enemies of the people," "*agents provocateurs*" belong in this division.

Terms of execration used among Communist factions are almost as numerous as those applied to class enemies. Among the older we find "Trotskyite" and "Titoist." Leon Trotsky was the Old Bolshevik leader who was second in command only to Lenin, but fell into disgrace, fled abroad, and was axed to death in Mexico by Stalinist agents; Tito, otherwise known as Josip Brož, leader of the Yugoslav Partisans who fought not only the Hitlerite invaders, but also Mikhailovich's pro-Western Chetniks, after collaborating with Stalin for a time in the attempt to communize Greece, broke away, established his own brand of "National Communism," and wound up by accepting both military and economic aid from the West; since that time a "Titoist" is a Communist who refuses to be a Moscow flunky.

Among choice terms of present-day "fraternal" Communist criticism are "diversionist," "revisionist," "deviationist," "dogmatist," "capitulationist." The first three mean that those guilty of the practices are straying away from the doctrines of the Four Evangelists of Communism (Marx, Engels, Lenin, Stalin). More specifically, the "diversionist" engages in disruptive tactics that may extend to the point of sabotage; the "revisionist" wants to change the sacred Marxist content (the term has been in use since 1865, but was redefined in 1958 in Moscow's *Political Dictionary*); the "deviationist" indulges in destructive internal criticism as he departs from party principles; the term is recent (1961). There is even "sectarianism," an old 1827 word, with the new charge that he who practices it wants to segregate himself from the toiling masses and set up what amounts to a "New Class." These charges are frequently leveled at the Russians by the Chinese. The Russians in turn accuse the Chinese of "dogmatism" and "doctrinarianism" (but these are old sixteenth-century terms), because the Chinese want to follow the gospels in fundamentalist fashion, and accuse everyone who wants to stray away from the rulebook of being a "wrecker" or "capitulationist" (Khrushchev, according to the Chinese, showed signs of wanting to capitulate to the West), thus threatening the "monolithic character and inviolable indestructibility of the socialist camp," and committing "isolated solidarity," "national egotism," and "power chauvinism." "Isolated solidarity" means that the Russians are deliberately and knowingly isolating themselves from the great National Liberation Movement of the underdeveloped nations, which is in the Chinese view the main source of world revolution today. The Russians retort with "Maotsetungism" and "Pekingese splitters." "Cult of personality" was one of the charges made against Stalin in 1956 by Khrushchev, and still to some extent deplored by Soviet leaders, who now profess to believe in "collective leadership." It is observable, however, that just as many images of Communist saints appear in Russian processions as in Chinese parades, though the stress is more on Marx and Lenin than on Brezhnev and Kosygin.

Two seemingly very recent additions to this terminology of ideological controversy are "democratic centralism" (this is interpreted to mean "control of the party") and "proletarian internationalism" (translated as "all must follow Moscow's lead").

It has perhaps been noted that the suffixes *-ism* and *-ist* play a large role in the Communist vocabulary. These are, of course, highly productive suffixes in many fields of ideas, and cannot really be accused of being Communist monopolies.

CHAPTER 17

The Vocabulary of Racial Relations and Racial Uplift

In a column entitled "A Word in Search of a Meaning," William Buckley explores some of the uses and connotations of the term "racist," tracing it back to Hitler, who, not satisfied with proclaiming the superiority of his own race, proceeded to exterminate others. Having heard the word used in connection with a man who had merely stated, with documentary evidence, that illegitimacy among blacks is higher than among whites, the Conservative writer offers various dictionary definitions of the term, and concludes that some verbal distinction ought to be observed between, say, Harry Byrd and Adolph Hitler.

During the 1968 pre-convention campaign, Governor Rockefeller, in his attempt to convince the Republican National Convention that the Republicans could win with him, but not with Nixon, called upon the latter to disavow any link with former Governor Wallace of Alabama, who, far from supporting Nixon, was running on his own ticket and damning both major political parties ("Have you stopped beating your wife?"). Rockefeller called Wallace a "racist." The term is fairly recent. The 1932 Oxford Dictionary offers neither "racist" nor "racism" (the second appears in the Addenda with the date 1942), though it states that "racial" has been in use since 1862, and suggests "racialist" as a possible derivative. Our more recent American dictionaries, Webster's Third of 1961 and the Random House Dictionary of 1966, offer both "racist" and "racism," deriving the second from modern French *racisme*. To Fowler (1931 version)

"racial," "racism," etc., are nonce-words, coined for a particular occasion; but the 1950 edition modifies this into "hy-
brids," on the ground that there is no Latin root for the base
word "race," which ought therefore not to be combined with
such established suffixes as -*al* and -*ist*. In this he is supported
by some Romance etymological dictionaries, which trace
"race" back to Old High German *reiza*, "line," but not by
others (notably Meyer-Lübke's *Romanisches etymologisches
Wörterbuch*), which claim Latin *generatio* as the source of
"race."

The modern definition of "racist" is, roughly, one who
advocates or believes in "racism," itself defined as the assumption that psycho-cultural traits and capacities are determined
by biological race, and that races differ decisively among
themselves; usually accompanied by a belief in the superiority
of a particular race and its right to domination over others.
The definition of "race" which applies is "stock characterized
by more or less distinct combinations of physical traits trans-
mitted in descent." This would seem to give "racism" some
measure of scientific standing, save for the assumed superiority and right to dominate. It would then have remained for
Rockefeller to prove that Wallace had claimed such superiority and right. Mere advocacy of racial separation would
only place Wallace in the same boat with the more extremist
wing of the black movement. Rockefeller might then have
reasonably been called upon to disavow any support from
the latter.

It might be added that the root-word "race," whatever its
origin may be, has given rise to many compounds, of which
one, "interracial," is surrounded by an aura of general approval, save in a few restricted circles.

"Racism" (or "racialism") seems to have become more
popular than an older set of words, which included "bigotry,"
"intolerance," and "prejudice," as well as the later "discrimination." Of course, the adjective "racial" may be used with
any of these terms.

The practices that all these terms refer to may be summarized by the outward manifestations of "segregation," a word that has given rise to such slang abbreviations as "seg" and "to outseg." (Someone was once described as "outsegging" Wallace.) "Jim Crow" is another term that describes the practice of keeping blacks and whites apart. It has the merit of being more specific. According to some sources, the term arose in the early decades of the nineteenth century, on Kentucky plantations, and was later used on the stage as the name of a blackface comic character. If this explanation is accepted, there is a ready-made semantic connection in the fact that a crow is black. However, the name "Jim Crow" has also been in use for an unspecified period of time in Worcestershire, England, where the expression "Jim Crow and Mary Anne" means "unsettled weather." This may be a pure coincidence.

"Apartheid," from Afrikaans, is a term sometimes used as a synonym for "racial segregation." It came to English in 1949, having been coined at an earlier date by South African Premier M. Malan, who justified it on the ground that it was an "inactive" expression, implying a state of affairs rather than an "active" practice, like "segregation" (the state of being apart, as against the act of separating). Like the derivatives of "race," all these terms are sometimes loosely used.

The remedy for a practice that has brought so much unhappiness to Americans, both black and white, is "desegregation," "integration," or "assimilation," words which perhaps hold slightly different implications. ("Desegregation" means doing away with the practice of segregation in general; "integration," to use Premier Malan's imagery, is a more "active" term, and implies more energy in bringing the races together and making them dovetail, if not mix; "assimilation" means "making alike," or absorbing a smaller group into a larger one, with implications of loss of cultural identity, something that many blacks resent.)

The "Reconstruction" that followed the Civil War ran

largely in the direction of conferring upon the liberated slaves political rights not previously possessed. The Civil Rights program which has been in progress for many years is designed to confer upon the black portion of our population some measure of equality, not only along political, but also along economic, educational, and social lines. It may be well to examine these segments in detail for their linguistic content.

The 1954 Supreme Court decision that marked the beginning of an effective Civil Rights program dealt specifically with the racially segregated schools of the South, which were ordered to desegregate "with all deliberate speed" (a somewhat weasely expression, since it lent itself to lengthy delays in compliance). This was a reversal of another decision rendered by the Supreme Court in 1896, which sanctioned "separate but equal facilities" (again a somewhat weasely wording, not so much for the "separate" as for the "equal"). In northern states, where the school system had long been theoretically desegregated, there arose a charge of "*de facto* segregation," caused by schools that served their own neighborhoods, particularly in the larger cities. "Racial imbalance" was claimed, and attempts were made to correct it, going far beyond the Supreme Court decision, with the forced bussing of pupils from one section of town to another for purposes of "racial balance." ("Imbalance," by the way, is so recent a term that it fails to appear in the Oxford Dictionary.) This proved highly impractical in many instances, both because of distance and traffic situations, and because many parents, both black and white, insisted that it was psychologically detrimental to young children to take them out of their accustomed environment and plunge them into a strange one in which they would feel themselves to be an isolated minority. Be this as it may, a new and opposite tendency began to develop, particularly in New York City, known as "decentralization," whereby in a given locality the schools would be locally run rather than administered by a large, impersonal, central Board of Education. (In practice, the schools would be staffed, preferably, with teachers of the same race as the pupils.) While this practice is still in the experimental stages, it must be pointed out that in effect "decentralization" works out very similarly to the "separate but equal facilities" of the 1896 Supreme Court decision, ruled unconstitutional by the 1954 Supreme Court. It should be obvious that we cannot both have our cake and eat it. The present Supreme Court is still to be heard from in the matter of "decentralization," but the point will doubtless be raised in the near future, as white teachers are excluded from predominantly black neighborhood schools with resultant disastrous teachers' strikes.

Another area where racial points of view sometimes clash is that of housing. Here the key word is "ghetto," flanked by "slums," and even by the euphemism "inner city."

"Ghetto" is an ancient word, first appearing in English in 1611. There is doubt whether it represents Hebrew *get*, "divorcement," or the tail end of Italian *borghetto*, "small city section," "little borough." Its original meaning is that part of a medieval city to which Jews were restricted; but the word was also used in the days of unrestricted immigration to betoken areas of American cities, particularly New York, where Jewish immigrants congregated in large numbers. Eventually the word acquired the sense of any city area where ethnic or racial groups reside in semi-isolation and under slum conditions. The most recent outcropping is the verb "to ghettoize," appearing in Webster's Third, but not in the Oxford Dictionary, in the sense of "to isolate," "to force to live in a slum." The word is occasionally used by hypersensitive writers and reviewers to refer to any separate mention of Jews or blacks, even where the mention is not at all disparaging.

"Open housing" is seemingly so recent that none of our dictionaries, including even Safire's work of 1968, report it. ("Open house," in the hospitable sense, is in Webster's Third and the Random House Dictionary, but there is no connection.) This is strange, because "open housing" bills and laws have been under consideration for some time, constituting the legalistic version of the earlier "block-busting." This was in origin a military term, referring to the giant bombs of World War II ("block-busters"), then transferred to the reprehensible practice of certain real estate firms of provoking panic selling of houses in certain neighborhoods by spreading rumors of black invasion and playing upon the fears and prejudices of white house-owners.

Very recently, there has appeared a shift of approach. While until recently stress had been on integrated housing, and large-scale acceptance of black citizens into white communities, many blacks now seem to prefer "Civic Action Programs" leading to broad improvements in their own predominantly black areas, with considerable pride in the "Black Community." "Demonstration [or "model"] cities [or "areas"]," combining integrated housing with local improvement of former black slums, seem, at least provisionally, to supply partial answers to many problems.

A third important area of racial unrest is that of economic opportunity, which is covered by Civil Rights legislation only to the extent that such legislation forbids discrimination in employment. Poverty as such lies beyond the pale of both race and Civil Rights. Before we touch it, we might examine some of the semantic implications and dictionary uses of "Civil Rights," "Human Rights," and "Civil Liberties."

The word "right" goes back to Anglo-Saxon *riht*, which in turn goes back to an Indo-European root **reg*, whose basic meanings are both "straight" and "king," and which has widespread ramifications. ("Rajah," "regal," "royal," "rule," "rich" are only a few of the words derived from this same source.) In the meaning in which it is applied in the two word groups in question, the Oxford Dictionary gives, among the uses that go back to Anglo-Saxon times, "that which is consonant with equity or the light of nature; that which is morally just or due"; also, "justifiable claim, on legal or moral grounds, to have or obtain something, or to act in a certain way."

What is difficult to find in the dictionaries is a clearcut definition of "human rights." This is perhaps due to the fact that the combination is, or should be, self-explanatory: those just claims which all men may advance. What these may be, however, is a matter of controversy. Should we settle for life, liberty, and the pursuit of happiness? Life is easy to define. Liberty is controversial. The pursuit of happiness is often an illusion, and just as often runs squarely into a violation of the real or alleged rights of others. Are property rights to be included among human rights? We would certainly reply in the affirmative, the Communists would just as definitely take a negative stand. What of the right to express one's opinion in speech or writing, commonly known as freedom of speech and of the press? What of the right to worship as one pleases (freedom of conscience)? What of the right to oppose the policies of the group in political control? What of the right to leave a country, a locality, an occupation, at one's own will?

It is of interest that the United Nations has, among its other activities, a Committee on Human Rights. Precisely which rights are considered human by the United Nations, and therefore subject to international discussion, is a matter concerning which most of us are in the dark. How human rights can profitably be discussed by an international body containing such contrary views concerning the relative status of the individual and society is somewhat of a mystery. Socialist country representatives may argue that all men are entitled to a job (what its remuneration shall be is a matter of individual discretion), to such benefits as social security, medical care, old-age pensions, and so forth. These are economic "rights," which might even be interpreted as not being inherent to the human being. Just how they can be fitted into the same pattern as the other rights mentioned above, the right to worship, to oppose, to resign and get out if one is dissatisfied, is altogether a matter of conjecture. It is little wonder that the dictionaries, even the new Webster's Third, shy away from giving a definition of "human rights."

For "civil rights" the situation is slightly better, though still quite confusing. The Oxford Dictionary mentions civil rights under the heading of "right," but merely to refer you to the adjective. Under "civil" we find no entry, save one that looks like an afterthought, under the main heading of "civil law"; this is defined as the old *jus civile* of the Romans, the law of all Roman citizens, but also as "the law of any city or state regulating the private rights and duties of its citizens." This rather hazy definition is paralleled by that of the older Webster, which does not handle civil rights as such, but states under "civil": "pertaining to a city or state, or to a citizen in his relations to his fellow-citizens or to the state; as *civil rights*." This seems to make civil rights a matter of individual discretion, depending upon the locality or the form of government, and this definition affords very little satisfaction to anyone. The 1961 Webster's Third offers a surprising definition of "civil rights": "those rights the enjoyment of which does not involve participation in the establishment, support, or management of government—specifically, the rights secured to citizens of the U.S. by the 13th and 14th Amendments to the Constitution and to [certain acts passed by Congress; these are specified by date] abolishing the civil incidents of involuntary servitude."

The first part of this definition seems to imply that civil rights do not include the right to register and vote; and even the second part, despite its clear allusion to two Amendments and a succession of acts of Congress, stresses the abolition of slavery more than anything else.

The 1966 Random House Dictionary, after bringing in the Amendments and acts of Congress, goes on to offer a second, *a posteriori* definition: "the rights to full legal, social and economic equality extended to Negroes." This is a practical, working definition, but still misses the philosophical point.

Are such rights to be extended only to Negroes? Do they not exist for the entire population?

It is fairly obvious that a satisfactory definition of "civil rights" does not exist. Perhaps it is time one were formulated. It would be good to have one that is a definition and not a slogan.

Should not the right to register and vote be made the subject of a clear, unequivocal statement, rather than of the weasel wording of the 13th Amendment, which merely threatens to curtail a state's representation if that state curtails the voting privileges of a portion of its citizenry? Ought not the right of free association, extending even to marrying whomever one pleases, be specified as a civil as well as a human right? Should not the right to use public educational facilities in accordance with one's mental equipment and preparation be made official, both in the law and the dictionary?

Conversely, by what mental acrobatics can one define as a civil right the correction of "racial imbalance" in schools which serve a district or neighborhood? Or the right to demand that a given race be represented in public or private employment in proportion to its numbers in the total population rather than in accordance with its capacity to fill the occupations in question? Or that a private employer be forcibly deprived of his right to choose whom he shall employ, however arbitrary the grounds for his choice? If these aberrations continue to be tolerated and encouraged, we may as well forget about all human rights, all civil rights, and all freedoms of the individual. Those who call upon the organs of government to assist them in securing this type of "civil right" should be the first to realize that they are advocating the abolition of another dictionary item, "civil liberty," which the new Webster clearly defines as "freedom from arbitrary governmental interference, specifically by denial of governmental power and in the U.S. especially as guaranteed by the Constitution." Civil liberty is the bulwark of protection not only for the individual, but also for minority groups.

The problem of poverty is only by indirection one that involves race. The great 1963 March on Washington was on behalf of civil rights alone. Johnson's "War on Poverty" began in Appalachia, and black poverty was only one of its many facets. But by 1968, when the "Poor People's March" on Washington took place, and Resurrection City was erected and torn down, the problem had somehow been shifted to the point where Dr. Abernathy's following consisted overwhelmingly of blacks, with a very sparse representation of Indians, Mexicans, and poor Southern whites. It was a melancholy episode, no matter which way you look at it, and one of which no American can be proud.

Linguistically, "poor," the key word, goes back to Middle English, having been derived from Old French *povre, poure* (modern French *pauvre*), which in turn goes back to Latin *pauper*. The formation of the Latin word itself is composite (**pau-per-os*, from *paucum* and *pario*, "little-producing," "one who produces little"). All our English dictionaries concur in defining "poor" as "having few or no material possessions; so destitute as to be dependent on gifts or allowances for subsistence; indigent; needy." An additional connotation is "mentally or morally inferior," "not worth much," which carries us back to the etymology of the Latin word. One element that fails to appear in etymological dictionaries is the fact that poverty is to some extent both relative and subjective. A Southern sharecropper, or a slum dweller on relief, is poor with reference to the great American middle class; he is affluent by comparison with the starving millions of some areas of the earth. The same sharecropper may refuse to consider himself poor so long as he manages to be self-supporting and may even hold out for middle-class status. (This phenomenon was actually viewed in a CBS television program entitled "Hunger in America.") Relativism in disposable wealth exists even in societies that label themselves "classless," and "the poor you have always with you" is Biblical. Differences in ways of easing and relieving poverty abound. For what concerns our American society, where by official figures no more than 25 per cent of the population may be described as poor by any standards, self-satisfied complacency is almost as dangerous as the current wave of hysteria. The poor, in such districts as New York's Harlem, upon being polled, give clear indication of their innate good sense. They rate the availability of jobs, decent housing, and educational opportunity far above more idealistic goals, such as complete social integration. They, of all people, should know what they need. At the same time, it is a national disgrace that an affluent society that takes it upon itself to lavish its food surpluses upon other nations for dubious political purposes should tolerate hunger and malnutrition in any of its own areas, however remote. Bungling administrations responsible for "Hunger in America" richly deserve to be replaced.

The slogans and epithets of the racial situation supply us with weasel words aplenty. Here we have the songs and chants of black demonstrators, ranging all the way from the beautiful old spiritual "We shall overcome" and Dr. Martin Luther King's "I have a dream" of 1963, through "Jim Crow must go!" and "Freedom Now!" (a rather bewildering slogan, since "freedom" was achieved over a century ago, and it is really other things that are wanted "now"), to the bellicose "Black Power" (1966) of Stokely Carmichael, discussed in the next chapter because of its sometimes violent implications, and the "We've got the white man on the run!" attributed to a highly placed black politician. On the segregationist side, we have "Never!" "White Supremacy," and "WASP" ("White Anglo-Saxon Protestant").

There is a choice vocabulary of obloquy on both sides, a good deal of which runs rather far back. "Darky," which our American dictionaries warn us is an offensive term, goes back to 1789, but was originally slangily applied to the night, then to a dark lantern. "Jigaboo" is another term at least equally offensive. (It is said to be a combination of "jigger," itself an insulting term, and "boo.") "Negro" is a borrowing from Spanish (1555), and means neither more nor less than "black." It lent itself to both southern and northern mispronunciations that carried contemptuous overtones ("Nigra," "Nigger"). For a while it was fashionable to replace it with the euphemism "colored" (internationally confusing, because in South Africa "colored" is applied not to blacks, but to East Indians and persons of mixed ancestry). Capitalizing "Negro" seemed for a time to remove the odium. Then other euphemisms appeared: "non-white," "member of a minority group" ("racial minority" usually means black, "ethnic minority" is European), even "Afro-American." The term that black Americans tend to prefer for themselves is simply "black," the Anglo-Saxon translation of the Spanish *negro*. Dr. King, in 1967, even coined the phrase "Black is beautiful," which indeed it can be. There seems to be no good reason why whites should not go along with this black preference, based on the fact that "Negro" is reminiscent of the days of slavery.

Disparaging black terms for whites are at least as numerous. Starting with the "poor white trash" and "Ku Kluxers" of the South, they go on to "whitey," "Mr. Charlie," "The Man," "pig." The last two, particularly the second, are often specifically applied to the police by Black Panthers and other Black Nationalist groups. "Pig," as a term of execration and loathing applied to human beings, goes back to 1596, but the identical use of "swine" goes back to earlier Middle English. "The Man" is identified by the Random House Dictionary as a term for employer, but no dictionary gives it as applied to police; the Random House is also the only dictionary to give us "man" as a common black exclamation and term of address. "Mr. Charlie" has two possible origins; one is its use in the sense of "night watchman," found in 1812, but supposed to go back to the days of Charles I, who founded a corps of night watchmen in 1640; the other is "White Charlie," a term applied to conservative Whigs in 1842. "Big juice" is occasionally applied to a white racketeer who enjoys police protection.

The use of a derisive "honkies" by the more radically inclined blacks to refer to whites of foreign extraction is countenanced by none of our dictionaries, though the American ones give the earlier "hunkies." The Random House Dictionary goes so far as to etymologize "hunky" into "Hung(arian)" plus "(don)key." There is a still earlier "Bohunk," said to be a telescoping of "Bohemian" plus "Hungarian," which was current in the days of a widespread immigration from southern and eastern Europe, and is recorded from 1914. Still earlier is "Hunker," applied to a conservative faction of the Democratic Party in the late 1840s. There seems to be no connection with "hunk" meaning "piece," derived from Flemish and in use since 1813, or with British "hunks" (crabby old man) of 1602, or with the 1861 "hunky" of "hunky-dory," which comes from a Dutch word meaning "goal," and was originally used in the sense of "safe on base." If we discount the Random House Dictionary's rather improbable link of "hunky" with "donkey," both "Negro" and "honky" are perfect illustrations of words that historically and etymologically are purely descriptive, and not at all offensive, but have been invested with unpleasant connotations through usage and misusage—typical weasel words.

There are some ingenious but misguided semantic shifts connected with the Civil Rights movement, so recent that they appear only in the latest of our dictionaries, the 1966 Random House. One is the use of "token" and "tokenism" to refer to those blacks who are fully accepted by and integrated into a predominantly white society. Here the base word, "token," goes back to Anglo-Saxon *tācen*, and has always carried the meanings of "outward indication," "symbol," or "metal piece used in lieu of money." The Anglo-Saxon word has for its Indo-European cognates Greek *deiknymi*, "to show," and Latin *dico*, "to say, tell." The novelty is in the peculiar application of the term in certain black circles. It goes hand in hand with other ironic expressions, such as "Uncle Tom," "Aunt Thomasina," and "Dr. Thomas," to describe those blacks who in ever-increasing numbers integrate.

Black writers speak scathingly of the practice of "creaming," the selection of the best-qualified black applicants for lucrative and responsible posts, in preference to less gifted and less prepared blacks. It may be pointed out that "creaming" is a universal practice, applied to white as well as to black applicants. Employers rather naturally prefer those applicants who are best qualified, and tend to reject those they cannot use.

A few other random terms from the vocabulary of racial relations include "second-class citizens," used as an example in Webster's Third, but not defined. This term may in practice apply to blacks, but in law it has more specific application to naturalized citizens, who cannot run for President, may be deprived of their acquired citizenship under special proceedings, and were until very recently subjected to various restrictions in the matter of foreign residence and travel which did not apply to the native-born: if they chose to reside abroad, they were required to come back to the United States periodically or lose their citizenship, and they were warned that the U.S. could not properly protect them under international law if they ran into difficulties, such as military draft in their countries of birth or even in the countries of birth of their parents.

"Backlash" is a term, borrowed from the vocabulary of mechanics and fishing, in the early 1960s, to signify adverse white reaction to Civil Rights movements, particularly as translated into votes at election time. "Frontlash," to betoken the opposite political phenomenon, was used by Lyndon Johnson in the 1964 campaign (he claimed three "frontlash" votes for every "backlash" vote), but seems to have originated with television commentator Roger Mudd.

The picturesque "soul brother" often used by blacks in

referring to members of their own race ("member" may be used as a synonym) goes back to a use of "soul" that arose in pre-Civil War days to describe feelings of strong sympathy on the part of northern whites with the plight of the slaves. "Soul" has become attached to a number of words, including "food" (dishes of which Afro-Americans are especially fond, including turnip greens, hominy grits, and chitlings, humorously dignified by the name of "ruffle steaks"). There is even Floyd McKissick's proposal to erect "Soul City" in North Carolina, as a project meant to demonstrate the ability of Afro-Americans to conduct their own affairs.

"White Hope" is a prizefighting term that came into use after Jack Johnson became world champion. It was used to describe each white aspirant to the title who came up and went down for the count of ten. It has now been out of style for some time by reason of the long succession of black titleholders, including Joe Louis, Sugar Ray Robinson, and Mohammed Ali.

There is even what might be described as a black National Anthem, "Lift Every Voice and Sing," composed by James Weldon Johnson.

CHAPTER 18

Burn, Baby, Burn!

The most doleful of our categories is that which has to do with violence and riots, whether of the racial or the educational variety. "Violence," which goes back to Middle English, is basically defined by the Oxford Dictionary and Webster's Third as "physical force, involving injury or damage to persons or property"; the Random House Dictionary more specifically defines it as "the unjust, unwarranted use of force exerted against the rights of others, or the laws."

To begin with, there is the "rumble," defined in our American dictionaries as a teen-age gang war, often involving the use of knives, zip guns, auto chains, and tire irons, with occasionally lethal consequences. The rumble antedates both black and student riots, though it sometimes had racial overtones (see *West Side Story*). It is described as a slang usage, with no known etymology; but the Oxford Dictionary gives us a possible source in "rumble-tumble" (1801), defined as "rough motion." Could this British usage have crossed the Atlantic?

"Riot" (1460) is defined by the Oxford Dictionary as "violence, strife, disorder, tumult, the outbreak of lawlessness on the part of a populace"; a rioter is one who "takes part in a rising against constituted authority." Webster's Third goes on to give a legal definition: "the assemblage of three or more persons for the purpose of committing turbulent, disorderly, unlawful acts." The Random House Dictionary adds the idea of "noisy, violent, public disorder." "Insurrection" (1419) is "a rising up in arms, an open revolt against authority." On this all sources are agreed. It may be recalled that in connection with the Detroit disturbances the use of "riot" as against "insurrection" to describe what was going on occasioned tragic delays in the use of federal troops. This was due to the provisions of insurance companies, which disclaim responsibility in cases of "insurrection." The difference seems to be of degree rather than of kind.

A somewhat similar distinction is made in the case of "murder" (a word of Germanic origin, but coming to Middle English through Old French), which is "the act of killing unlawfully, and with malice," and "assassination" (1618; but "assassin" goes back to 1531), which is "killing by treacherous violence, often through a hired emissary or a fanatical adherent to a cause." The Oxford Dictionary and Webster's Third, but not the Random House Dictionary, add the concept that the victim is often a public personage. The original assassins were the Moslem *hasheesheen*, or hashish eaters, who under the influence of the drug would set forth to kill Crusader leaders. This detail is presumably what adds the touch of the public figure to assassination, but not to murder. It is of interest that the Romance languages have merged the two concepts. When French demonstrators call Lyndon Johnson or General de Gaulle *assassin*, they do not mean that either President has murdered, or caused to be murdered, leaders on the opposing side; quite the contrary; the supposed victims belong to the anonymous masses. Therefore, the proper translation of the French slogan is "De Gaulle—murderer!"

But political assassination (as of the Kennedys or Dr. Martin Luther King) goes to join violence and crime in arousing, both here and abroad, a slightly hysterical impression that such things are peculiar to America and its structure. The student riots at the Sorbonne and the University of Mexico were bloodier and more violent than anything we have witnessed here, even at Berkeley and Columbia. Germany, Italy, Japan, Korea, Brazil, Belgium, Holland, Sweden have had their bloody student riots. Political assassination, in addition to running back at least to the days of the Gracchi and Julius

Caesar, has in this century had spectacular exemplifications abroad: the assassination of King Humbert I of Italy; that of King Milan and Queen Draga of Serbia; that of the Archduke Franz Ferdinand at Sarajevo, which led to the outbreak of World War I; that of the French President and the King of Yugoslavia in Paris; that of Count Folk Bernadotte in Israel; that of Mahatma Gandhi in India. Surely all these countries were not under the influence of violent Western films at the time of their occurrence. The contemporary American spirit of contrition for violence seems to be an extension of the "We are all guilty" complex. Perhaps "We were all brainwashed" by our news media and propagandists would be a more suitable slogan.

The New Violence, and the frequent assassination of public figures, has led to a strong agitation for "gun control laws" on the federal plane. There seems little question that mail-order interstate sales and shipments of arms might profitably be subjected to such control, though it might be pointed out that the federal government already has powers over interstate commerce, and apparently has not seen fit to use them. Beyond this, what control is wanted that cannot be more effectively exercised by the states? In New York, where there is a very stringent Sullivan Law against concealed weapons, crime flourishes. The criminal, being what he is, does not feel bound to obey any law. The law-abiding citizen, who might well use a weapon in self-defense, is told to rely on the police, who are not always on hand. In states like Idaho and New Mexico a rifle or shotgun is a necessity, not a luxury, to a rancher. In these days of rampant crime, might it not rather be expedient to issue permits and even instruction in the use of arms to all applicants who have a clean police record, with special encouragement to more likely victims of criminals, such as bus and taxi drivers, bank clerks, and storekeepers? Might not this type of gun control prove to be precisely the sort of crime deterrent that is needed? Bystanders are often criticized for not interfering when a crime is committed under their eyes. How many are so courageous as to oppose, unarmed, a vicious thug who is, or might be, armed? Does anyone seriously contend that the assassins of the Kennedys or Dr. King would have been deterred from committing their spectacular crimes by the fact that they could not acquire a gun legally?

In theory, the opposite of "violence" is "non-violence." The trouble with non-violence is that all too often it goes to join its opposite. Even abstracting from the use of "non-violent" in the names of groups pledged to burning and killing, we find a curious discrepancy between the definition offered by the Random House Dictionary ("refraining from the use of violence, as in reaction to oppressive authority") and that of Webster's Third ("peaceful but passive resistance and sabotage"). "Sabotage" starts out with its etymological meaning of throwing a shoe into a piece of machinery. It goes on to acquire the meaning of any deliberate act of destruction. Its more recent derived meaning of "an act of obstruction" makes no non-violent sense if the action is carried through to its logical conclusion. If I am running out of a house that is on fire, and you deliberately set out to obstruct me, it stands to reason that I'll knock you out of my way. Will your reaction then be a non-violent one? Sabotage entails violence.

Another expression in vogue is "civil disobedience," though both its component parts go back to Middle English. The expression was apparently not in general use at the time of the compilation of the Oxford Dictionary. Webster's Third defines it as "the refusal to obey the commands of government; non-violent, collective means of forcing concessions from government." The Random House Dictionary goes on to "refusal to obey the laws, including boycott, picketing, and non-payment of taxes." Once more we are left in doubt as to where non-violence ends and violence begins, and what the interplay of action and reaction may be. How non-violent can you get in the process of disrupting a city's or country's normal activities? If the laws are to be enforced, is it possible to have "civil disobedience" without violence and bloodshed?

More definitely on the non-violent side are expressions like "peaceful demonstration," not defined, but given as an example in the Random House Dictionary. The peaceful demonstration has such slogans as "Ban the Bomb" and "Make love, not war," though at times it turns more definitely political ("Dump the Hump"). There is, on the other side, "law and order," to which often is added a codicil, "with justice." There is also the large and growing -*in* family, which glorifies demonstrations under the names of "sit-in," "teach-in," "study-in," "mill-in," "kneel-in," even "love-in," and "sleep-in." (The last two have free-love sexual overtones.) The ancestor of all these popular expressions seems to be the old "sit-down" strike, which is fully described by both Webster's Third and the Oxford. "Teach-in" and "kneel-in" are so recent that they appear in neither of the older dictionaries. (The Random House Dictionary, however, defines "teach-in" as a prolonged series of lectures and discussions carried on as a protest against the Vietnam war.) "Sit-in," though absent from the Oxford Dictionary, is given by the Random House Dictionary; in Webster's Third it follows the verb "to sit in," meaning at first to take a hand in a card game, then "to participate" in general. As an adjective, it means "occupying a seat in a racially segregated establishment in order to register a protest." All seem to be legitimate coinages, whatever one may think of the practices they denote. "Involvement," which in Webster's Third definition is equated to "complexity or confusion," in the Random House Dictionary to "engaging the interest or emotions," seems to be a prerequisite to all the foregoing activities.

Until rather recently, the most strongly stressed part of the vocabulary of violence were the words and expressions of repression and reaction, as well as of white prejudice. Here

we encounter such generic terms as "fearmongers," "hate
mongers," "hate groups," even "hatenanny," coined on the
analogy of "hootenanny." "Ku Klux Klan" is a term that
goes back to Reconstruction days. Great doubt prevails as to
its etymology. One ancient theory was that the "Ku Klux"
portion was onomatopoetic, imitating the sounds of the cock
ing of a musket. Another jocular hypothesis was to the effect
that its initials, "KKK," stood for illiterate spellings of "Kikes
Koons, and Katholics," the three avowed foes. The Random
House Dictionary is the only one of our sources to venture
the idea that the first two words may represent Greek *kyklos*
"circle" or "group" (the same word that gives us "cycle")
with the Scottish "clan" added; but this would make it repe
titious. More recent are George Lincoln Rockwell's "Ameri
can Nazis" and the "Minutemen," which only the most recent
of our dictionaries, the Random House, gives as the name o
a group pledged to resist with force of arms any Communis
invasion or uprising.

On the other side, we have the "Freedom Riders" of the
early Civil Rights movement, but while there is record o
violence being visited upon them, the converse does not seen
to be true. The name was based on the analogy of the "Free
dom Fighters" of the Hungarian revolt against Communism
but the Freedom Riders were groups, usually mixed, who in
vaded the southern states from the North to urge southern
blacks to register, vote, and otherwise proclaim their new
status as full first-class citizens.

Two terms that often appear in connection with the Civi
Rights movement have heavily aggressive overtones. They are
"militant" and "activist." The first appears in late Middle
English in the sense of "one engaged in warfare or strife." By
1603 the watered-down connotation of "combative" is added
A figurative religious use appears in "the Church Militant."
By 1610 the original adjective appears used as a noun. Web
ster's Third defines "militant" as "aggressively active in a
cause," and exemplifies with "militant suffragist." The Ran

dom House Dictionary adds "vigorously active, aggressive, striving." "Activist" seems to be of recent origin, though "act" and "active" go back to Middle English, and ultimately to Latin *ago*, "to do, act." Here Webster's Third is quite specific: "advocating vigorous action, such as the use of force for political ends"; while the Random House Dictionary speaks more mildly of "an especially active or vigorous advocate of a political cause." Both words are quite elastic; neither is reassuring.

Pure black groups whose names, as well as programs and activities, arouse legitimate misgivings are the "Mau Maus," "Black Muslims," and "Black Panthers." The first take their name from a secret Kikuyu organization of Kenya which did not hesitate to massacre white settlers as well as other blacks in that country as they struggled for independence from British rule, which they finally achieved. The American organization is so recent that our American dictionaries give the term only in its African connection. The Black Muslims follow the Islamic faith and believe in full and complete separation of the races; their principles are generally lofty, and violence is advocated only in self-defense. The same applies, at least in theory, to the Black Panthers, who have been accused of aggressive tactics against the police, particularly in the Oakland section of California; they are listed in none of our dictionaries.

Among the slogans of black violence is "Long, Hot Summer," taken from the title of a Faulkner novel of 1958; its implication is that riots and violence will take place in the course of the summer, when tempers run high. "Burn, baby, burn!" is a cry often heard in the course of riots in black sections of American cities. But black sociologist Adrian Dove informs us that it had been used previously in connection with singers, who were urged by their audiences to improvise. The Rev. Adam Clayton Powell at one time gave an address in which he urged his followers to substitute the far more constructive, "Learn, baby, learn!" and "Earn, baby, earn!"

"Black Power," first circulated, if not coined, by Stokely Carmichael in 1966, is so recent that it appears in none of our dictionaries. When it eventually does appear, it will pose serious problems, in view of the various definitions and interpretations that have already been offered. The best link seems to be with another recent combination, "White Power Structure," which again does not appear, but is taken to mean "the group at the top that wields power over the society of which it is a part." Safire describes "Black Power" as "a deliberately ambiguous Negro slogan, meaning anti-white rebellion to some, the use of political and economic 'muscle' to others." *The New York Times* views it as four different things: pride in race and organization for political and economic action; an anti-white rallying cry; a paramilitary slogan leading to riots and rebellion; a chant that will ultimately take the Afro-American back to his African "homeland."

But rebellion against constituted authority has two additional prongs, which somehow seem to be related—the "Hippie" movement and the "Student Revolt."

"Hippie" is so new in our vocabulary that it appears in none of our sources, not even the 1966 Random House Dictionary. ("Hippy," of course, is "supplied with abundant hips.") Missing also are the "flower children" and the "Yippies," described in the press as the more militant and activistic of the hippies. (Again, "yippie" appears, but only as an ejaculation of triumph; the name "Yippies," however, is derived from the initials of "Youth International Party.") Best guess for "hippie" is that it goes back to "hip," a variant of "hep." ("To be hep" is to have awareness of something or other, most of all the inspirational qualities of jazz and other cacophonies.) But we have gone a long way since the days of the "hepcats."

Hippies and Yippies carry us on by easy stages to the "Student Power" which goes to join the now impressive list of creations that started with Carmichael's "Black Power." A magazine writer even suggests that "Woman Power" be used to clear the air of violence on television, guns in the household, pornography on the newsstands, and many of the other ills that afflict our "Sick Society." Perhaps so. They didn't call it by that name back in the days when "Votes for Women" were going to usher in a bright new day in national and international politics.

This entire concept of "Power" for a minority, whatever it may be, can be run into the ground. How about Italian Power, German Power, Polish Power, Scandinavian Power? Or Catholic Power, Protestant Power, Jewish Power? Or Teacher Power, Doctor Power, Engineer Power? Minority group "Powers" could range all the way from the Anti-Defamation League of the B'nai Brith to a nationalistic sublimation of the Cosa Nostra. Isn't it about time for the plain American majority to stress its power, at the polls if nowhere else?

Some of the minority group "power" manifestations seem to be of suspicious, even foreign origin. "Underground," first appearing in 1571 as an adverb, meaning "below the surface," moves on around 1632 to "in secrecy, in a hidden or obscure manner." There were various European undergrounds during World War II, which struck valid blows on behalf of freedom. Today the term is acquiring a more unsavory meaning. Webster's Third calls it a "clandestine conspiratorial cell or organization set up for revolutionary or other disruptive purposes." The Random House Dictionary calls it a "secret organization to fight an existing government."

One recent episode seems to have escaped general notice. Early in 1968, there appeared in New York subway stations a large advertising poster showing a booted, hooded, graceful, flower-carrying Russian ballerina. The only words on the poster were in Russian: "*Soyedinyaetes' k Podpolyu!*" To those who were familiar with Russian (but certainly not to the general public) the meaning was startlingly clear: "Join the underground!" Did the government authorities have any light to shed on this strange piece of advertising, designed only for the linguistically and politically hep (or hip)? It was meant to announce a new *avant-garde* periodical, we were told. Nothing to worry about. Maybe not. Still, one wonders. It was not too long afterward that we witnessed the seizure of a certain university by a small group of subversive students, and later of an educational television station (WNET) by an even smaller group of subversive hippies, who identified themselves to the startled television audience as "members of the underground." Mere coincidence, of course! Still, would the authorities have reacted with the same unconcern if a similar public announcement had been sponsored by the Klan, the Minutemen, or even the legalistic John Birch Society?

The Civil Rights and student movements have given us a number of semantic shifts. There is, for example, the slogan combination "police brutality," now often invoked in justification of "civilian review boards." (Such a board, first suggested in 1966, and sponsored by Mayor Lindsay, Senator Javits, and Senator Robert Kennedy, was overwhelmingly voted down in New York City.) It is interesting that the two-word combination appears in none of our major dictionaries, though the individual components do. "Brutality," entering the language in 1549, is at first a quality of animals, but becomes a human attribute by 1641. "Inhuman," "savage," "grossly ruthless," "devoid of mercy" are among the definitions. In the absence of any indication as to the origin or first use of the combination, all I can say is that it first came to my notice in connection with a televised broadcast of a congressional hearing on subversive activities several years ago. There were loud protestants among the audience. When sergeants-at-arms undertook to remove the disturbing elements by force from the chamber, those ousted somewhat triumphantly took up the chant: "Ah! Police brutality!" This long antedated civil rights marches or riots. It would therefore seem to have been borrowed by the more activistic wing of the Civil

Rights movement from earlier subversive movements. It may be added that while it is undoubtedly a much overused slogan, such a thing as police brutality exists and is occasionally in evidence, though not nearly as frequently as some would have us think.

"Crime in the streets" is of comparatively recent origin, as against the older "organized crime." While crimes committed in the streets go back to ancient history, the use of the modern cliché is claimed by some to betoken a state of mind, with perhaps a hint of racial overtones. Proof of the fact that "crime in the streets" is a very ancient phenomenon is spectacularly supplied by the etymology of "to cry" and all related Romance verbs (*crier, gritar, gridare,* etc.). The etymon is Latin *quiritare,* to shout *"Quirites!"* ("Citizens! Help!") when one was attacked in the streets of ancient Rome.

CHAPTER 19

The Tongues of Labor Relations

Some years ago, a large and powerful corporation, which shall here be nameless, asked me to make a study of the language of trade unionism as exemplified in the weekly periodicals issued by the two unions that represented most of the corporation's workers. The study was a revelation to me as well as to the corporation's officials. Here was weaselry at its best and finest, with every technique of propaganda abundantly illustrated: constant repetition; the use of special words, generally of a violent connotation ("smash," "blast," "hurl," "clamp," "smear," "break," "rip," "shatter," "crush"); the constant surrounding of certain words with specially selected modifiers calculated to arouse hostility ("profits," for example, were invariably "fat," "bloated," "fabulous," "gluttonous," "enormous"; "management" and "bosses" were "vicious," "arrogant," "unfair"; "interests" were "vested" or "special"; "corporations" were "soulless"); this practice was carried on to a point where mention of the noun would automatically bring up the modifier, in the same fashion that "Nixon" brings up "Richard," or "Charta" calls for "Magna"; distortions of meaning ("liberal" equated to "pro-labor," union indoctrination described as "educational campaign").

Once this study had been completed, and properly circulated in mimeographed form, I was requested to do a similar study of the management publications, which were under the direction of a particular pugnacious, aggressive editor, who did not at all hesitate to give tit for tat. Here were the selfsame practices, indulged in by the other side. Union doctrines were described as "pernicious," "destructive," "poisonous"; union claims were "untrue," "absurd," "wilfully misleading," "rabble-rousing"; union leadership was "inept," "selfish"; strikes were "long," "bitter," "misconceived," "ill-advised." Shop stewards were "trouble-making zealots."

"American" and "un-American" were very liberally sprinkled throughout, as was "free" in connection with markets, initiative, way of life. Profits were now "adequate," "reasonable," "just." "Losses" and "break-even points," which had been non-apparent in the language of labor, were very much in evidence in that of management. There were slogans such as "Big progress and big business go together," reminiscent of Charles E. Wilson's "What is good for General Motors is good for the nation." Capitalism was "enlightened," business practices were "sound and humane," corporations were "progressive," employees were "share-owning." This study, too, was mimeographed and circulated, so that the spokesmen of management would be able to guard themselves from falling into the same obvious semantic pitfalls as their opponents.

The corporation paid me generously for my two studies. In view of what I learned about the use and misuse of language, perhaps I should have paid them.

There are words and expressions which, together with the practices and institutions they betoken, are sacred to labor unions. The list begins with "labor" itself, which is surrounded with an aura of reverence not only by union members, but also by politicians who seek that elusive something known as the "labor vote." Unlike Britain, where "Labour" has turned into a political party (the political use of "Labour" and "Laborite" goes back to 1903), America has no labor party. It does, however, have powerful labor-union organizations, such as the AFL-CIO, the Teamsters, the United Mine Workers, the Automobile Workers of America, which are parapolitical, can swing elections, and often do, though perhaps not as often as their leaders would like us to believe. The labor vote is quite important, particularly to the Democrats. Terms like "workers" and "wage earners" are viewed with favor, both by labor and the politicians. So is "economic justice."

"Solidarity" is an old labor term that goes back to 1848, the year of big political and social upheavals in Europe. It may be paraphrased as "sticking together." In practice, it means that members of one union will not cross the picket lines set up by another union, and will in all other ways show their sympathy and support for their embattled comrades. One trouble with the word is that it has been to some extent taken over by subversive elements, so that labor is not quite as fond of it as it used to be. "Unity" is preferred. The "picket line" is the most sacred of labor's sacred cows. Once it is there, no union member may cross it. "Picket," a Middle English word ("picket fence"), began to acquire a military connotation in 1761, and was taken over by labor in 1867. One present-day darling of labor unions, particularly Walter Reuther's, is "guaranteed annual wage," which management is reluctant to grant without some corresponding sliding scale designed to offset possible losses. Sacred also is the "check-off," defined by our modern American dictionaries as the compulsory and automatic deduction of union dues from wages due to the workers, a practice so convenient and satisfactory, at least to its beneficiaries, that it was taken over by the federal and most state governments in connection with the income tax.

"Collective bargaining" is one of the most popular terms in labor relations. "Bargain," noun and verb, comes into Middle English from Old French *bargaigne* and *bargaignier*, which have to do with a market, an agreement, or a contract. Beyond that, there is disagreement among the authorities; some carry the word back to Germanic *borganjan*, which in Anglo-Saxon development gives us "borrow," others to Latin *barca*, "boat, skiff" (**barcaniare*, a hypothetical Vulgar Latin word meaning "to handle the boat in such a way as not to upset it with all who are in it"; there is in use today a popular Italian *barcamenare*, "to handle a boat," which has only the figurative meaning of "to get along; to exercise due tact and diplomacy"). The noun *bargayn* appears in Middle English, while the verb makes its appearance in the fifteenth century; in 1596 it definitely means "to chaffer or haggle." As applied to labor relations, it is only the 1961 Webster's Third that gives us all the ramifications, indicating that these usages are recent. "Bargaining power" is described as "the relative power to compel agreement on one's own terms"; a "bargaining unit" is "a group on behalf of which a union seeks to negotiate collective agreements"; "collective bargaining" is "any union-management negotiation." Here the objection (and it is a mild one) is to the extension of a term that originally means to discuss on a *quid pro quo* basis ("I'll give you two dollars for that steak"; "No, I want two and a half") to a procedure that normally involves ever-growing demands on one side, resistance on the other; while the consumer, who does not sit at the bargaining table, plays the role of forgotten man until it comes time to foot the bill. In the final analysis, the "collective bargaining" of the labor world does not differ too much from the "negotiations" of the diplomats.

Labor shares with finance and government administration a noun, "benefit," that looms large both in welfare work and collective bargaining. Stemming from French *bienfait*, which in turn goes back to Latin *bene factum* ("well done"), it first appears in Middle English, but only in the sense of "act of kindness or gift, something personal." It is transferred to the economic field ("what promotes welfare," "profit") in 1512. By 1911 it assumes a new nuance, "pecuniary help in time of sickness and old age." Its late appearance in this connotation explains why we do not find it in our 1884 Webster's, but the Oxford Dictionary shows that Britain shares it with us. It is now applied not only to favorable provisions of insurance and annuity contracts, for which one pays out of his own pocket, but also to Social Security, welfare and relief handouts, and to those clauses which labor unions manage to squeeze out of management (as in "fringe benefits"). Since by virtue of its original use it applies to something you get for nothing, I am inclined to question its semantic validity in connection with those fields where there is a *quid pro quo* (insurance and annuities primarily, union contracts perhaps).

An intriguing negative adjective that plays a big role in labor parlance is "unfair." Its affirmative form, "fair," goes back to Anglo-Saxon *faeger*, and means, among other things, "pleasing to the eye, beautiful, gracious, ample, light in color, characterized by honesty and impartiality." The negative form arises only in 1713, and is restricted to the sense of "unjust, using trick or artifice, dishonest, not equitable in business dealings." By 1886 it invades the field of labor relations and gets to mean specifically "paying below the normal wage-scale." Terms that are absent from the older Webster's and the Oxford Dictionary but appear in the 1961 Webster's are "unfair labor practice," "unfair list" (this, consisting of employers described as "unfair," is compiled by a union and used as a blacklist), and even "unfair trade practice," designed to get around business competition. Since in the minds of most people the old generic concept of "unfair" as "unjust" still prevails, it must strike many innocent victims of a labor stoppage, particularly in the service fields, as incongruous to see pickets carrying the "unfair" sign when they reflect on how unfair it is to be deprived of subway or bus transportation, elevators, hospital service, schools, heat in the midst of a winter flu epidemic, even decent burial, because the union members want a wage increase or a thirty-hour week while they, the victims, have to toil from forty to sixty hours to make a living. In these cases, proper semantics would dictate that the "unfair" poster be indeed displayed, but by the long-suffering public, and directed indiscriminately at both the union and the management that care nothing about the public's convenience or safety. There is no reason whatsoever why the word "unfair" should remain a labor-union monopoly.

An additional double term mustered from the field of labor relations is "round-the-clock negotiations" to "beat a strike deadline," as exemplified by what goes on every two years in New York public transportation. These are old, tired expressions reflecting a mentality and methodology that should long ago have been outmoded and outlawed. Why the deadline? What is wrong with uninterrupted negotiations until an agreement is reached, with retroactive provisions or some other sensible device to ensure justice to both sides and, above all, no damage to the long-suffering public and the national economy? This ultimatum system of conducting labor relations should have been effectively legislated out of existence at least half a century ago, and would have been but for the response of politicians to labor-management group pressure. Linguistically, our dictionary definitions of "beat" do not include examples connected with deadlines, save for Webster's Third. "Deadline" itself is defined as a "fixed time limit for finishing something." But when the word first appeared, in 1860, it had a far more literal meaning: a line around a military prison which could not be crossed by a prisoner under penalty of being shot dead. Appropriated by the journalistic world, the word lost its spatial connotation and acquired a temporal one. Still later came its take-over by the labor unions in connection with strikes.

All these are terms of which labor more or less approves. Others are "living wage," "standard of living," "working conditions," provided labor can supply the definition. The "closed [or "union"] shop" is also favored. Ultimately comes the "strike." "Strike" is a word with an interesting history. It goes back to Anglo-Saxon, but its use in labor relations began in 1810. The Oxford Dictionary reminds us that at the outset "strike" was often followed by "of work." There is no unanimity for this concept among Western languages, save for

German, which seems to have borrowed its word from English (*Streik*). Italian *sciopero*, from Latin *ex-opere*, "away from, out of, work," is fairly literal. Spanish *huelga*, from Vulgar Latin *follica*, *follicare*, goes back to the concept of "fool," "playing the fool," later turned into that of "loafing" (*holgazán*, "lazy," "do-nothing"). French *grève* comes from the name of the spot where striking Paris workers congregated, the Place de la Grève. Russian *zabastovka* is from the somewhat mysterious root *bast-*, which does not appear in other words. (In any case, Russian workers are not allowed to strike, so the term is academic.) A management euphemism for "strike" is "volume variances from plan."

"Moonlighting" is a term that has recently been introduced to signify working on a part-time job at the same time that one holds a regular, full-time position (as a New York policeman who, with the full approval of the authorities, drives a cab during his off hours, thus helping to discourage hold-up men who prey on taxi drivers at the same time he earns a few much-needed extra dollars; unfortunately, he sometimes makes up for lost sleep on his tour of official duty). The Oxford Dictionary defines it as a term used originally in street lighting, but other sources report that it was used around the 1880s in connection with Irish-peasant night raids against obnoxious landlords, and that another term, "smooting," was in use at that time for the double occupation.

Terms that are to organized labor as red rags to a bull include the "Taft-Hartley" Act of 1947, and its "cooling-off period" before a strike can be declared (the latter term was used earlier, however, in connection with international tensions); "speed-up," defined as increasing the worker's output with no corresponding increase in wages; and "right-to-work laws" ("union busting" is the term preferred by labor), which are state laws banning the closed or union shop, where only regular, dues-paying members may work. "Profits," as we have seen, are regularly surrounded by unpleasant modifiers in labor usage; the word goes back to Middle English, but has been applied in the financial and labor fields only since 1604. "Layoffs," "lockouts," "sweatshop conditions" come in for their innings.

The practice of "strike-breaking," another term of loathing, has as its appendages some choice terms for those who engage in it by working during a strike or ignoring picket lines: "scab," a word from Scandinavian, first appearing in Middle English in the sense of a crust that forms over a healing wound, begins to be applied in labor relations in 1590; the connection is obscure, and the British often prefer an older term, "blackleg"; the American use of "scab" goes back to 1811. "Rat," another ancient word, becomes anthropomorphic in 1788 for one who deserts his party ("Rats leave a sinking ship"), and finally acquires its labor use in 1881. "Fink" is a mystery word, which some attribute to German-Yiddish, others to Scandinavian influence; it is said to be connected with "finch," and the word was at first used in connection with an informer, one who "sings" to the police; it is now applied also to a strike-breaker. "Lackey," an all-purpose word meaning "servile follower," and occasionally used in labor relations to describe those workers who are disposed to go along with management, has been in use in English since 1529, and goes back to Arabic *al-kaid*, the same word that produces Spanish *alcalde*, "mayor." "Company birds" and "stooges" are two slangy replacements for the above terms. Management, by the way, normally consists of "leeches," "tycoons," "magnates," "privileged minorities," and "coupon clippers."

Management revels in such terms as "people's capitalism," "free economy," "free (or "private") enterprise," "incentive system." It also likes "protection," involving tariffs that, by artificially raising prices on imported goods, make it possible for uneconomic American producers to stay in business; it is one of the few terms, incidentally, that are favored by both capital and labor, since it fosters full employment. "High wages," "excellent working conditions," "generous benefits (or "settlements")" are also on management's approved list. (Suitable adjectives for these nouns in labor's vocabulary are "pitiful," "slave," "substandard," "miserable," "inadequate.")

Among terms of execration widely used by management are "unreasonable demands," "gouging practices," "demagogic leadership," "questionable political affiliations," all of which are attributed to the unions; the last term is a polite way of calling a labor leader a Communist without laying yourself open to being sued. Men on the picket lines are sneeringly referred to as "picketeers." Management's biggest bugaboos are "featherbedding," not reported by the Oxford Dictionary but defined in the American dictionaries as labor practices designed to force the hiring of more workers than are needed, or the forcible retention of workers whose jobs have been rendered obsolete by automation; and "wildcat strikes," which come about without the permission of the union officials or a regular strike vote; the name seemingly goes back to "wildcat" oil wells (1812), which gush when they are not wanted to.

"Big" is a term that is applied indifferently to business, labor, and government, though only the first of the three combinations appears in our dictionaries as a separate item. In labor parlance, business is unalterably and irrevocably "big." The practice of replacing "horizontal" trade unions (running across a given trade or occupation through many plants) with "vertical" ones (running through an entire plant or industry with all its different categories of workers), along with the fact that unions are not yet subject to anti-trust laws, probably led to the coinage of "Big Labor." "Big Government" is, of course, too well known to require discussion. Perhaps a fourth power should be added to the list: "Big Consumer," or "Big Public," or "Big Voter." But that requires organization, and most people just won't organize.

CHAPTER 20

Economic Jargon

Some years ago the *Guaranty Survey*, a monthly review of economic and business conditions published by the Guaranty Trust Company of New York, came out with an article entitled "Semantics as an Economic Weapon," which was widely copied and quoted in the financial pages of various newspapers. It was the author's contention that those who wish to be informed rather than exploited by what they read or hear must be constantly on their guard against the hidden implications in words.

The article began by drawing attention to the subtle distinctions implied in such terms as "rolling adjustment," "disinflation," "unboom," "readjust," "dip," "deflation," "boom and bust," "recession," "depression." The important differences among these terms lie not so much in their expressed meanings as in the emotional responses their connotations arouse in reader or listener, responses which as often as not are wholly subconscious, and therefore all the more dangerous.

Advocates of government involvement in the economy do not normally advocate "inflation" or "deficit financing," because these are "fear" words. What they urge instead is "public works" and "tax relief," which alarm nobody; in fact, they conjure up visions of more money in everybody's pocket, along with fine new roads, schools, hospitals, playgrounds, and what have you.

"Chronic inflation" would imply a slow descent into monetary debasement. But a "gradual increase in prices and wages" connotes larger incomes and good times for all.

Economic quackery, said the article, is betokened by such terms as "rationalism," "planning," and "the scientific approach to economic and social problems." They parade the professional knowledge of the speaker or writer and belittle the intelligence of anyone who questions his views. But actually there are no "experts" in the field. Far too many of our economic woes can be traced to "centralized planning." Eternal vigilance against the beguilement of words is the price of liberty, the article concluded.

Not to be outdone, the financial columnists pointed out that what was once known as "boom and bust" is now a "business cycle," with "rolling readjustments"; that good old "supply and demand" had given way to the "administered prices and wages" of a "managed economy," which calls for high output and prices for commodities for which demand may be meager, merely because it suits the purposes of the administration's domestic or international policies.

Where stock market prices once "skidded," now we have a "technical correction," or even a process of "preparing the base for a new rise." "Motivation" has been devised, in the form of polling the citizens as to why they buy or fail to buy. After all, there is a "full-employment commitment," and we must honor it. Or, if you prefer, the administration makes the commitment and the rest of us have to honor it.

But there are many other sectors where the government and its economists display their weaselry in action. It has been noted that while the military branch of government deliberately underplays its vocabulary, the economic sector is flamboyant and prone to exaggeration. Here are such loud-sounding phrases as "overheating economy" and "gross national product." New taxes are justified not on the basis of the government's needs for its multifarious activities at home and abroad, but on the ground that the economy is "overheating" (whatever that may mean), and that we must "siphon off excess purchasing power" (what excess purchasing power?) under penalty of "inflation," which for once is described as "impending" and "disastrous." But an "expanding" or "booming" economy is what our modern school of economics has been advocating for years and decades ("a little inflation," like a modest dose of pregnancy, "does not really hurt"); and the government has been going along with all sorts of built-in inflationary provisions: farm price subsidies, minimum wage laws, higher Social Security payments, Medicare and Medicaid, educational grants, failure to control either prices or wages. It isn't really fair to pour money into people's hands and then want to siphon it off. A milder substitute for "overheated" or "overheating" economy (none of our dictionaries recognizes the combination, by the way) is the earlier, optimistic "expanding economy." Here it is amusing to note that at a United Nations committee meeting, the Soviet delegate took violent exception to the term as it came out in his translated version ("self-expanding economy" in Russian). He pointed out that an economy, particularly of the capitalistic variety, could not possibly be self-expanding; someone would have to expand it. The point was rather well taken.

"Gross national product," on the rise of which so many rosy hopes are predicated, is an American invention. The Oxford Dictionary defines the three words, but not together. The Random House Dictionary equates it with "the total monetary value of all final goods and services produced in the country in a year." If we deduct an allowance for depreciation of capital goods, we have a "net national product." There is a third term, "national income," which is defined as "the sum total of wages, salaries, rents, dividends, and interest." Webster's Third has a strikingly different version of "gross national product": the total value of goods and services, including total expenditures by consumers and government, plus gross private investment. Here the key phrase seems to be "expenditures by consumers and government." This is at loggerheads with "goods and services produced." There is a secondary contradiction between "services" and "produced" or "product." Services are not produced, but rendered, and no product results from a service, such as the barber cutting my hair or the delivery boy putting the paper on my porch. But if we accept the Webster's Third definition of "gross national product," our basis is expenditures, not production, or even service-rendering. These expenditures include not merely those of the consumers, but also those of government, which are superlatively non-productive. We can double our welfare payments and send the gross national product spurting skyward. We can lavish a few more billion dollars on foreign aid, and obtain the same result. "Gross national product" is one of the most weasely of weasel expressions ever coined. The word "product" lulls you to sleep; it makes you think we are producing more, when we are merely spending more. There is a parallel in the inclusion of Secretary Freeman's "concessional exports" (those for which we don't get paid, like wheat to India or Egypt) in our plethoric excess of exports over imports. As our synthetic prosperity dwindles, along with our gold reserves, it is to be hoped that the voters will finally awaken to the phoniness of the terminology (and concepts) of our government economists.

All this illustrates the governmental interference with both economic process and economic vocabulary that has been going on since the early days of the New Deal. But a good deal of our economic-financial terminology is traditional, and far antedates Roosevelt's administration and the succession of Presidents, slogans, and measures that followed it.

Consider, for example, such terms as *laissez-faire*, which started with the French eighteenth-century economists, crossed over to England in 1825, and received full citizenship in the vocabulary of political economy in 1887; or "Surplus Value," which was Karl Marx's term for what we would call "profits" (the difference between the wages paid to the workers and the final value of the goods produced); or the "cutting of melons" (paying out extra dividends), which goes back to 1908; or the "supply and demand" economic theory of 1776. Even the pre-1929 stock market knew such expressions as "cats and dogs" (wildcat stock issues), "blue chips" (common stocks of the most stable corporations), "equity (or "venture") capital" (that part of a corporation's capital which comes from the sale of common stock). "Good (or "bad") for business" is a very old phrase.

"Free market," "free enterprise," have been around quite a while. So has "reconversion" (1611). But "recession," while quite ancient in other acceptances, did not come into the financial field until 1949, and then only in the United States, and usually accompanied by the adjective "temporary," to remove some of its sting. On the other hand, "depression" applied to business conditions is exemplified from 1793 on. "Inflation" goes back quite a way, but its synonymous opposites, "deflation" and "disinflation," date back only to 1919 and 1947, respectively; the coinage of the second in spite of the existence of the first seems to point to a governmental-economist vogue of the prefix *dis-*, of which other examples appear. "Incentive" is a fairly old term, but its opposite, "disincentive" (a measure meant to discourage production) dates from 1951. One term so recent that we cannot find it in any dictionary is "dismerger," the opposite of the established "merger." "Freeze" (in the sense of "price-and-wage freeze") dates back only to 1949. Our "crash" has not crossed language boundaries, but "crack," which we do not use in a financial sense, has. Both French and Italian use *crac* in the sense of "business failure," "bankruptcy," and the term has occasionally been used in both languages to denote a stock market crash.

Very recent creations of the financial world are "conglomerate" and "give-up." The first is used to describe large and important mergers of many corporations whose activities are altogether diverse—for instance, Canada Dry, *McCall's* magazine, and one or more food industries; or the merger of Hertz Rent-a-Car with RCA and a few other big firms; the formation of "conglomerates" is often due to special tax situations, where the losses of one member cancel out the profits of another, so that a tax saving results. Even "mini-conglomerate" has begun to appear in financial pages. "Ghettonomics" is another very recent term, coined to describe the science of taking care of the economic and financial needs of the big city ghettos. "Give-up" describes a fee-splitting practice whereby mutual funds that market their securities through brokerage houses require the latter to give back part of their commission (often as much as 50 to 70 per cent), either to the managers of the funds or to other brokerage houses in which the managers or the funds hold an interest. This makes the financial "give-up" the equivalent of the more popular "kick-back." The legality of the practice is beyond our scope or depth. Quite slangy is the use of "headhunter" to describe a firm's agent who acts as a talent scout for likely executives. Then there is the very recent vogue of "crunch," which has been extended to the credit field ("credit crunch" instead of "credit squeeze").

There are in the financial world a few taboos, terms that are normally avoided save in special connections. As has been seen, "inflation" is seldom used by the administrations that bring it about, being replaced by euphemisms (unless it is desired to scare Congress into passing a tax hike); but when used by foes of the administration, it is usually attended by unsavory modifiers. ("Creeping," "galloping," "built-in," "chronic" are among the favorites.) "Capitalism" is normally avoided, save to make a special point ("People's Capitalism," for instance). This is due to the fact that our good Communist friends have invested the word with so many ugly connotations. Use instead "free enterprise."

Some financial terminology is confusing to its own users. "Security," for instance, is a word that appears in a military connection ("national security"), in a widespread sense ("old age security"), and in a stock market use ("a list of securities held for your account"). "Recap," legitimately used in connection with automobile tires, becomes an abbreviation for "recapitulation," but is also used by financial circles for "recapitalization," though this appears in none of our dictionaries.

Other economic terms bewilder those who approach our language from the outside. "Net worth," in the sense of a person's net assets is bad enough (Webster's Third defines it as the excess of resources over liabilities, and the Oxford Dictionary exemplifies the expression from the writings of Steele); but what is the foreigner to make of the question "What is he worth?" which he will interpret in the sense of "How good, how trustworthy, how reliable a man is he?" rather than "How much money does he have?" Yet "to be worth" is listed in our dictionaries as "to have property." The Oxford Dictionary informs us that "net," meaning "free from deductions," goes back to 1500, while "worth" is Anglo-Saxon for pecuniary value. Its interchangeability with "high value" or "excellence" begins in 1617, but its application to a person goes back to 1591; its application to possessions (1592) is said to be obsolete or archaic; but "of material value," "capable of being estimated in terms of money" goes back to Middle English. The confusion seems to arise from the interchange of "worth" with pecuniary value on the one hand, with personal valor or moral qualities on the other. The impression these twin expressions create in the non-Anglo-Saxon mind is that speakers of English consider money to be the measure of a person's value to society.

A large segment of our economic and financial terminology is not merely government-inspired, but government-dictated. This is due largely to the ubiquitous influence of the income tax, which causes most financial transactions to be predicated upon their tax effects. Such terms as "capital gains," "depletion allowance," "non-profit corporation," "tax-exempt," "tax-deductible" are illustrative of the way in which the government octopus fastens its tentacles not only on the economy, but on the vocabulary as well. If you can turn an item of income into a capital gain, your tax liability is normally much smaller. (When Eisenhower wrote *Crusade in Europe*, he called the money he got for it capital gains, and made it stick; but the average author is not advised to try it.) "Depletion allowance" means, at least legally, a reduction in the capital value of something you own that results from consumption; this favors Texas oil barons, but not people who wear out their bodies and brains working for a living. If one can turn a productive enterprise into a "non-profit" corporation, he can pay himself a liberal salary, but will find his business exempt from corporation taxes. Churches and church organizations, colleges and universities, scientific, educational, and charitable bodies of all sorts and descriptions and particularly foundations are normally tax-exempt, and anything that flows into their coffers, whether it be the result of outright gifts or of related business activities, such as apartment-house rents and spaghetti factories, has no taxes charged against it. But in addition, gifts made to such religious, charitable, scientific, or educational organizations are declared tax-deductible to their donors. Since every cent the government fails to collect from one group of taxpayers has to be made up by other groups, this means in effect that the modest wage-earner is forced to subsidize churches, colleges, and foundations, whether he believes in them or not, while the man who endows a foundation and retains control over its activities is able to subtract from taxation all the money he pours into it. Add to this that the taxpayer who has no foundation at his command may heartily disapprove of some of the things the foundation does (at his expense), but is powerless to do anything about it. The Ford Foundation, for example, subsidized the experiment in school "decentralization" that led to the series of New York City teachers' strikes in 1968. Also, a fund-raiser for a non-profit, tax-exempt institution can truthfully tell the millionaire whose contribution he solicits that if he gives a thousand dollars to his favorite charity, he will in effect be giving only $100 to $500 of his own money, and "the government" will contribute the rest, since he will drastically reduce his tax liability by reason of his contribution. "The government," in this instance, happens to be the rest of us. The identical principle applies to the inheritance tax (what our British cousins more brutally call "death duties").

Add to this that on the basis of tax-deductibility as applied to business enterprises there has come into being a giant network of expensive industries (travel, hotel, restaurant, entertainment, radio, television, magazine advertising) that prosper on the principle that if a corporation does not get rid of some of its surplus profits on padded expense accounts and costly advertising, "the government gets it anyway," and the weaselry of "tax-deductible" becomes very evident. Yet any attempt to remedy this situation would throw our economy into a tailspin, by reason of the far too many vested interests that are involved—not merely the industries themselves, but the millions who derive employment and a livelihood from them. Verily, Alice's Wonderland had nothing on us.

One last and more cheerful area in our exploration of economic and financial jargon is supplied by a combination consisting of a stockbroker (Albert Haas) and a psychologist (Don Jackson), who have discovered a link between stock market operations and sex. They speak of a period of flirtation and anticipation before the stock buyer moves, since timing is as essential in stock trading as it is in romance and sexual conquest. Then comes the moment of fulfillment—profit-taking—followed by the customary relief and afterglow. The two writers point to the sexual overtones in some of the stock market's terminology: "make a killing," "selling climax," "breakthrough," "fill or kill," "straddle," "to violate the lows." Last of all, they point to that symbol of both sexuality and stock market optimism, the bull. It may be well to leave the subject on this "bull" note, while we are ahead.

CHAPTER 21

The World of Euphemisms

Newsweek once came out with an unsigned article entitled "Never Call a Spade a Spade." This drew my attention at first because of the popular saying in its title. It was a reminder that different languages express similar philosophical concepts in different words and with different imageries. "To call a spade a spade" would come out in most Romance languages as "to call bread bread, and wine wine." However, I found the contents of the article equally entrancing. They dealt with the world of euphemisms, where "people expressways" is used for "sidewalks," "automotive internist" for "automobile mechanic," "activity booster" for "pep pill," "creative conflict" for "demonstration," and where a frankfurter becomes a "tube steak" while a hamburger, after going through a "Salisbury steak" phase, turns into a more modest "chopped steak." In Pentagonese, "disposal center" means "junkyard."

What is at the root of euphemisms? At first glance, one would say that it is the desire not to shock or offend. This is particularly in evidence in connection with expressions dealing with sexual activities, bodily functions, parts of the body, even conditions such as drunkenness, for which Benjamin Franklin once drew up a list of 228 euphemisms current in his day. (Wentworth and Flexner give an up-to-date list of about 500; "pixillated," for example, starting in the United States in 1848, with the original meaning of "dazed," "befuddled"; "wiped out" is very recent; "wiped over" seems to be a transferred surfing term.)

Is there something more? Particularly, is there something that may justify us in placing euphemisms in our weasel-word category? I believe there is. It is a desire to be thought better, more refined, more cultured, more sensitive, more polite than you really are that causes you to speak of a man being "intoxicated" rather than "drunk," of a woman being "expecting" rather than "pregnant," even of a bookmaker "making book" instead of "laying odds." "Lubritorium" is so much more learned a word than "service station," and "lubricate" sounds better than "grease."

A colleague of mine once wrote that if you say "I ain't" in certain milieus you won't be invited to tea again. Since you do want another invitation, you repress what may be your natural tendency to say "I ain't" and use "I'm not" or even "aren't I?" in the interrogative instead. This puts what the Communists would call the profit motive, or, to be euphemistic, the "factor of economic determinism" into our linguistic behavior, and this is where the weasel element comes into the picture.

In previous chapters we have seen euphemisms aplenty, many utterly harmless, others calculated to achieve an effect. When the telephone company changed its "information" to "directory assistance," they probably meant to bring to your notice the fact that they were helping you out, something that should have been obvious to you in the first place, but which you might be taking for granted. When the "Internal Revenue Bureau" became the "Internal Revenue Service," they were getting away from the notion of bureaucracy, which for many has unpleasant associations, and putting in the pleasant word "service," with its implication that they were doing you a favor by taking your money. Similar euphemisms, by the way, appear in other languages; what we rather brutally call a "taxpayer" in English is known in Italian as a *contribuente* or "contributor"; he is not just paying out his life-blood to a soulless government; he is contributing to running the nation; he pays just as much, but it makes him feel good. In like manner, a French speaker pays out his *contributions* to his government. "Human Resources Administration" is the New York City politician's way of describing an obvious present liability which only the most optimistic can view as a potential future asset.

While euphemisms appear in every corner of language, there are certain fields where they are almost mandatory. In medical parlance, for instance, they may not replace "death" with "passing away" or "passing on," as is done in lay circles, and there is on occasion a brutal phrase such as "mercy killing" (but also the euphemistic "euthanasia"). But consider also such terms as "neoplasm," in use since 1864, which literally means "new growth," but in effect means a tumor (not necessarily cancerous, by the way); the patient who would be scared to death by "cancer," or even "tumor," often takes "neoplasm" in his stride. "Inoperable," in use since 1886, means just what it says; "terminal," in scientific use since 1825, but recently extended to mean "occurring at or contributing to the end of life," sounds less drastic. Yet you may be able to live on with an inoperable disease, but not with a terminal one.

The term "doctor" itself is in a way a euphemism, because etymologically it means "teacher" (Latin *doceo*, "to teach"); this is reflected in "Doctor of Philosophy," which is, in the words of a West Virginia mountaineer, "a teach-doctor, not a real doctor." "Physician" is more to the point, since he deals, etymologically at least, with your physical or bodily self. On the analogy of "physician," however, "mortician" was coined in 1895 to replace a less pleasant sounding "undertaker" (less pleasant only by reason of familiarity; a "mortician" deals specifically with the dead; an "undertaker" merely conducts you underground). Later, around 1926, even "beautician" was coined as an added euphemism for a beauty-shop operator.

Nowhere are euphemisms more in evidence than in the

related fields of bodily organs, bodily functions, and sexual manifestations. There is no point in going into all the elegant, scientific-sounding replacements for the so-called "four-letter words" (itself a euphemism) which everybody knows and which are so unnecessarily stressed in many modern plays, works of so-called literature, and political demonstrations. There is, however, a phenomenon that might be called euphemism in reverse, which few are aware of. Look up the etymological derivation of "pencil" and "orchid," words that have never impressed you as having any kind of questionable connotation, and you will see what I mean.

An entire chapter could be written about the incredible euphemisms created in all languages, from ultra-civilized English and French to the Pidgin of the Melanesian islands, for what might be styled, euphemistically, a "rest room." The British "convenience" and "cloak room," the French *les W.C.* (the abbreviation stands for a borrowing from an earlier English expression, "water closet"), the Italian, Spanish, and Russian words that literally mean "retreat" or "retiring place," the German "away-place," the Melanesian "house-peck-peck," are only a few samples. "Toilet" itself comes from French *toilette*, "little piece of cloth."

There are euphemisms for normal and abnormal sexual relations, for the possible outcome of the former, for the people who indulge in either or both. "Have fun" may be invested with overtones at the adult stage that it would not have if addressed to a child. The frank "pregnant" may be replaced by French *enceinte*, by the Italian loan-translation "to be in an interesting state," by the smart-alecky "lady in waiting," or by an "expectant" that has been in circulation since 1862 for a father, being extended to a mother only twenty years later. The uneuphemistic and thoroughly traditional term, by the way, is "with child."

The verb "to sex" has been observed in a newspaper headline that ran "Girl sexed to death"—a rather brutal euphemism, but a euphemism nevertheless. "Sex" as a noun has been in use

since Middle English, and since 1631 in what the Oxford Dic
tionary describes as the "class of phenomena with which thes
(anatomical) differences are concerned." As a verb it appear
in 1884, but with the meaning of "to determine the sex of, t
label as male or female." Webster's Third, however, gives u
"sex up" with the meaning of "arouse, increase the sex appea
of," and the Random House Dictionary gives the euphemisti
"coitus" for the noun, and "to sex it up" as a verb.

Where an American police or newspaper account will stat
that a murder victim was sexually "molested," the Britisl
story will say she was "interfered with," an expression tha
our American dictionaries do not present in that meaning
The Oxford Dictionary offers "interfere with" as stemming
from 1632, but defines it as "to meddle with a person withou
having the right to do so." This sends you scurrying on t
"meddle," where you discover that "to meddle with," fron
Old French *mesler*, "to mix, mingle," goes back in a sexua
connotation to 1655. The American-favored "molest" goe
back to 1494 in the (British) sense of "to meddle with a per
son in such a way as to cause injury." Webster's Third define
"molest" as "to meddle or interfere with a person withou
justification and from sexual motivation." The Randon
House Dictionary limits itself to "making indecent sexua
advances." "Molest" carries the much milder etymologica
meaning of "trouble," "annoy," and the picture it conjure
up in the minds of speakers of languages that stem more di
rectly from Latin is one of mild annoyance, such as woulc
be caused by a gadfly or a bore (witness the Italian religiou
admonition *sopportare le persone moleste*, "to bear up witl
people who bother you"). All of the English expressions are
misleading, and might profitably be avoided by the use o
something like "assault" or "attack" if the more serious mean
ing is intended.

"Abnormal," "queer," "homo," "deviate," "transvestite" are
often used in describing homosexual practices. "Homo" is a
mere abbreviated form, defined as colloquial by the Oxforc

Dictionary and as downright slang by Webster's Third and the Random House Dictionary; it lends itself to confusion with the masculine "homo" of "homo sapiens." "Queer," slangiest of all, had an original British euphemistic use as "drunk"; the American application is described as having arisen in the 1920s among hoboes. "Abnormal" is a euphemism pure and simple, since abnormality might apply to any item of behavior. "Deviate" has been in English use since 1560, but the Oxford Dictionary does not report it in the sense under consideration, while Webster's Third and the Random House Dictionary agree in defining it as "sexual pervert." "Transvestite," not given by the Oxford Dictionary, appears in both American dictionaries as one given to wearing the garments of the other sex, and only by implication does homosexuality enter the picture. "Poof" for "homosexual" sometimes appears in British usage.

More remotely associated with sexual euphemism are terms like "streetwalker," "whoreson," and "ecdysiast." The first, a demure synonym for "prostitute," has surprisingly been in English usage since 1592. The second was recently resurrected by an elegant writer who wanted to call someone by the term for which the euphemistic abbreviation "s.o.b." is generally used; it goes all the way back to Middle English, arising as a loan-translation from Old French *filz a putain*, which means exactly that, and is described by all dictionaries as obsolete or archaic for "bastard." But "bastard" is another euphemism, from Old French *filz de bast*, "pack-saddle child." Here Webster's Third speculates that *bast*, "pack-saddle," may come from the Germanic root that gives us "barn." The Random House Dictionary prefers to view the *bast* as a makeshift bed. A third possibility is that the illegitimate child is likened to a pack-saddle-bearing mule, the "illegitimate" offspring of a horse and a donkey. "Ecdysiast" is an elegant Greek euphemism for "strip teaser," derived from *ekdyo*, "to shed, remove clothing." The Oxford Dictionary does not report it, but gives "ecdysis," the shedding of a snake's skin or a crustacean's shell. An equally elegant euphemism is French *effeuilleuse*, "one who sheds leaves," as do trees in the fall.

Two additional expressions in the field of sexual euphemism are "parietal rules" (college regulations concerning sleep-ins among students of different sexes), and "to relate to each other as human beings," where the basic meaning is obscured to the point where we are not even certain that a sexual connotation is meant. There is also the very recent "hung," used by Gore Vidal to denote "equipped with male sexual organs" ("well hung").

That English is perhaps more given to the practice of euphemism than are other languages seems indicated by the word commonly used to replace "drunk." The etymological meaning of "intoxicated" is "poisoned"; yet from its earliest appearance in the sixteenth century English speakers have been applying it to those who are under the influence of alcohol. Though we may be right and all others wrong, we are the only ones who spare the feelings of our drunks by saying that they are "poisoned."

Three additional euphemisms connected with drinking are "grocery," which in parts of the South often means "saloon" or "bar" (for this there is a curious parallel in Spanish *bodega*, which generally means "grocery store" in Latin America, but "wine shop" or "saloon" in Spain; witness Blasco Ibáñez' *La Bodega*); "ordinary," which in Virginia and in parts of Britain has the meaning of "inn" or "tavern" (the Random House Dictionary calls it "obsolete," while the Oxford Dictionary gives its first appearance in this sense as occurring in the United States in 1774); and "package store," often used in New England for "liquor store."

Coinages, Actual and Suggested

To the extent that a coinage is designed for a specific purpose, it may be described as a weasel word. The weasely effect
may be publicitarian and commercial, political, literary, intel-
ectual, or any of a dozen other things.

Coinages are as often as not anonymous. They generally fit
into one of two major classes: compound words, of what
Lewis Carroll called the "portmanteau" type, which gather
two meanings into one form, often with telescoping of the
two words into each other; and derived forms, where a prefix
or suffix is joined with a root word to form a new word. Only
occasionally do we get a created grammatical form, like the
spurious past tense "shat" employed by Gore Vidal in his
Myra Breckenridge, and previously by Mary McCarthy in
The Group.

Typical of coinages that have already entered the language
are the "smog" that was produced back in 1905 by combining
"smoke" and "fog"; the "mattergy," combining "matter" and
"energy," occasionally used in scientific circles, but unre-
corded in our dictionaries; the very popular brood of an
original "motel" ("motor" plus "hotel"), which has gone on to
give us "boatel," "floatel," and other similar forms. One such
coinage, offered by E. J. Steichen, which has not yet taken
hold but should, is "grismal" ("grim" plus "dismal"), descriptive of certain days. Another, offered by a columnist for what
passes for fiction in certain circles, is "pornovel." Still another
is "astrodoggle," offered by W. Howard for a space boon-
doggle. Lastly, there is "girlcott," humorously coined on

the analogy of "boycott" by Walter Kiernan of WOR to describe a type of activity that women initiate.

Occasionally there is compounding without telescoping. A columnist recently offered "househusbandry" to describe the sort of family situation where the husband stays home and attends to the domestic chores while the wife goes out to earn their joint living. Other columnists have offered similar creations, such as "Popspeak" and "Rockspeak." The first is merely "popular speech," while the second refers to the political talk indulged in by Governor Rockefeller and his aides during the 1964 campaign to shorten long political cliché ("bomfog" for "brotherhood of man, fatherhood of God"; "moat" for "mainstream of American thought"; "fisteg" for "fiscal integration"; "govelop" for "government closest to the people").

Typical of the derivation process are such forms as "Great Societese," to describe the language used by Lyndon Johnson and his cohorts in pushing our recent political fad, and "Vietlish," which sums up the type of language induced by the Vietnam war.

Another example, offered by a California correspondent, is "hecticity," more elegant, perhaps, than the "hecticness" recognized by our dictionaries to describe a state of hectic activity. "Hectic," by the way, comes from Greek *hektikos*, which in turn comes from *hexis*, "habit"; it has been used since 1642 in English to describe the constant, habitual fever that attends consumption. (Italian uses *etico* exclusively to denote "consumptive," running into confusion with another *etico* that means "ethical"; this is what happens to languages that drop Greek *h*'s.) The Oxford Dictionary gives "hectic" in the sense of "stirring, exciting, disturbing" since 1904, but labels it "colloquial."

Other forms that have recently appeared in the press are "communauts," to describe people who travel tens of thousands of miles commuting, and "astronautrix," for a female astronaut.

Encouraged by the success of these creations, I should like
o submit a list of *desiderabilia*, words that do not yet exist,
ut for which there seems to be a call. If there is a bit of
weasely *arrière pensée* in my behavior, I stand ready to take
ne consequences. "To rambunct" and "to connipt" would be
sable verbs coined by what the linguists call "back-forma-
on," from "rambunctious" and "conniptions."

For suffix formations, I should like to offer "jackassical,"
intellectuous" (with its noun derivative "intellectuosity"),
nd "squzzly." The first seems called for as a stronger syn-
nym for "asinine," combining as it does the qualities implied
y another adjective, "mulish"; it could be applied in situa-
ons where stupidity and obstinacy blend to produce dire
esults, as in the sphere of foreign policy.

"Intellectuous" and its accompanying noun in *-osity* could
vell be used to describe what is pseudo-intellectual, particu-
rly in the literary, artistic, and musical fields, as well as the
ort of pose that is struck by some of our more pompous
cholars and know-it-alls.

"Squzzly" could be well applied to pets, and might be
oined by a verb "to squzzle." Here you both "squeeze"
gently, to be sure) and "cuddle" the aforesaid pet. The word
r words would be a boon to cat and dog lovers, and analogi-
al justification is supplied by "squshy," which already ap-
ears in our dictionaries.

"Screechy" is a term that already appears as an adjective.
n my opinion, we should use the well-known process of
unctional change to extend it to a noun use, for application
o those female singers who think that volume makes up for
onal quality, and wax so enthusiastic over their torch songs
hat they force us to turn down the set to save our eardrums
nd sanity.

A loan-translation from Italian *smidollati*, "unmarrowed,"
ould profitably be applied to members of our hippie genera-
on who lack both guts and a purpose in life.

Lastly, there is the entrancing possibility of a vast extension of *sex*-portmanteau forms, for which a precedent already exists in "sexploit" and "sexploitation." Consider the potentialities of "sexport" for those glamour actresses who come to us from overseas; of "sexplosion," to go along with all the other explosions that brighten our days, and for which there is undoubted justification in the current state of our *mores;* of "sexperience" for the sexual experience that so many of our college students of both sexes revel in; of "sexpensive" for what costs money in the field; of "sexclusive" and "sexgregation" for what has so often been advocated for schools where integration is feared by reason of its overtones of miscegenation.

This, of course, is only a beginning. But it is a fair sample of what can be done with language if one really tries.

APPENDIX B

Prefixes and Suffixes

It should be fairly obvious to the reader who has advanced this far that from the vast lists of prefixes and suffixes offered in such works as those of Partridge and Wentworth and Flexner there can be culled a certain number which seem particularly adapted to the formation of weasel words, lending themselves to purposes of propaganda, irony, fun-making, thereby betraying, at the very least, a weasely frame of mind on the part of those who overuse them. Accordingly, without any reflection upon our predecessors (Partridge tried to give us a comprehensive listing of all prefixes and suffixes in the language, while Wentworth and Flexner made a fairly successful attempt at collecting such linguistic forms as are favored in slang), we should like to offer two lists that seem to predominate in our chosen field.

For weasely prefixes, we would nominate the following:

anti- —Greek for "against." This is the prefix of opposition *par excellence*, and appears particularly in connection with political and social movements, but may extend to other fields as well (witness "anti-personnel weapons"): "anti-labor," "anti-Saloon League," "anti-Defamation League," "anti-Semitic," "anti-anti-Communist."

dis- —negative and separative prefix from Latin; more active and dynamic than *de-*, and accordingly favored by government bureaus and business organizations that like to stress activity ("disinflation," "dismerger," "disincentive," "dissaver").

219

mega- —Greek for "big, great"; used scientifically ("mega volt"), but also humorously, by scientists ("megabuck," "megamistake," "megatonnage").

mini- —from Latin *minor*, "lesser, smaller," or *minimum* "least," possibly with influence from "miniature"; very recent vogue started by "miniskirt," which appears in none of our dictionaries, not even the 1966 Random House; goes on to many other fields ("minicast," "minicrisis," "minilove," "minicourse").

neo- —Greek for "new"; does not in the least detract from its more popular Anglo-Saxon counterpart ("New Left"), but is favored by the more intellectuous artistic and political element ("neo-Classicism," "neo-Plasticism," "neo-Fascist," "neo-Nazi").

non- —negative prefix from Latin. Seems to deny or negate what follows, but does not always function as it should ("non-resistance," "non-violent"). Is in competition with *un-* (*q.v.*).

sch-, schm- —borrowed from Yiddish and applied indifferently to Yiddish loan-words and to native forms; conveys a faintly contemptuous note ("schmo," "schlemiel," "schnook," "schnozzle," "schmear," "schmeetings").

ultra- —Latin for "beyond," "extremely"; much used in political parlance ("ultra-conservative," "ultra-liberal"). May on occasion be replaced by the adjective "extreme" ("ultra-right-wing," "extreme right wing").

un- —from Anglo-Saxon, negative and privative, equals "not"; currently very much in vogue, and used in practically all fields ("un-American," "uncollege," "unCola," "unhep," "unboom," "unthink," Walter Lippmann's "unpoor, unyoung, unblack"; we might even add "Students for an Undemocratic Society").

Over- and *under-* might be added to the list, save that they
re far too generalized, often used with weasely connotations
"over-" or "undersexed," "oversized," "overlearn," "over-
ompensate," "underdeveloped," "underprivileged").

Our list of nominations for suffixes:

cade—originally from "cavalcade," then extended by pub-
citarian interests to such forms as "aquacade," "motorcade,"
tc.

r, -est—the normal comparative and superlative suffixes of
nglish adjectives, but extended commercially to nouns
"coffee-er," "macaroniest").

eria, -eteria—originally from the ending of Spanish *cafeteria,*
o indicate a place where goods or services may be procured,
ften with a self-service feature ("booketeria," "valeteria,"
fruiteria").

eroo—originally from "buckaroo," which seems to go back
o Spanish *vaquero,* "cowboy"; slightly contemptuous, and
avored by stage and screen circles ("flopperoo," "bunkaroo,"
switcheroo").

ie (often replaced by *-y*)—diminutive, often used in pet
ames and other endearments, favored in baby-talk and by
he feminine sex ("birdie," "dearie," "hanky").

in—the Anglo-Saxon preposition of location, currently used
o denote gatherings, usually for protest-demonstration or
exual purposes ("sit-in," "teach-in," "mill-in," "be-in,"
love-in," "sleep-in"). Said to have originated as a prefix in
in-gathering," an eighteenth-century revival meeting.

ism—a highly intellectual suffix from Greek *-ismos,* denoting
eligious, political, philosophical, artistic, or ideological belief;
nuch used in Communist circles ("Titoism," "Trotskyism,"

"revisionism," "Gaullism," etc.). Changed to -*ist* to denote the person who practices the -*ism*.

-*ize*—from Greek -*izein*, infinitive suffix; a favorite among bureaucrats, who use it to coin unnecessary words ("finalize," "definitize," "containerize").

-*nik*—from a Russian suffix of agent; vogue probably started by Sputnik; tremendous political extension ("Vietnik," "peacenik"); but also in other fields ("dogoodnik," "lunik," "Beatnik," "holdupnik," even "neatnik," "nudenik," "strikenik," and "SFnik" for "science-fiction writer"). Russian *kukuruzhnik*, literally "corn-nik," "hick, rube," might be profitably borrowed, since it would fit in well with our own use of "corn" and "corny." The labor movement apparently borrowed "sabotnik," which is used to indicate a celebration in someone's honor. There is doubt whether the root word is French *sabot* ("wooden shoe," which gives rise to "sabotage") or Russian *subbota*, "Saturday."

-*ology*—Greek -*logia*, from *lego*, "to speak"; widely used in science and philosophy, occasionally extended to form words that have a slight weasely flavor ("ideology").

-*phobia*—from Greek *phobos*, "fear"; often humorously used by intellectuals ("treiskaidekaphobia," "fear of the number 13"; "phobophobia," "fear of fear itself").

-*rama*—originally from -*orama* of "panorama," "all-view" (Greek *orao*, "to look at"); commercially extended to forms like "motorama" and "telerama."

-*thon*—from the Greek place name Marathon, site of a victory over the Persians and starting place of a messenger's race to bring the news to Athens; extended from "race" to include any form of protracted activity ("danceathon," "telethon," "talkathon").

-*ville*—from the French word for "city"; used by blacks and

ive musicians to denote either a place or a situation ("Soul-
ille" for Harlem, "Cornville," "Moneyville," "Feelsville,"
ven "Bombsville" for something that is a "bomb" [howling
uccess]).

Index of Persons, Titles, and Things

The author wishes to acknowledge his indebtedness to his many sources. First among these are the three standard dictionaries used in this study: *The Shorter Oxford English Dictionary* (Clarendon, Oxford, England, 1955 ed.), *Webster's Third New International Dictionary* (G. & C. Merriam Company, Springfield, Massachusetts, 1961 ed.), and *The Random House Dictionary of the English Language* (New York, 1966). These are so often referred to in the text that it would have been impractical to list page references for them in the following index. Four other works less frequently mentioned are indexed under the entries "Partridge" (Eric Partridge, *Origins*, The Macmillan Company, New York, 1958), "Wentworth and Flexner" (H. Wentworth and S. B. Flexner, *Dictionary of American Slang*, Thomas Y. Crowell Company, New York, 1960), "Safire" (William Safire, *The New Language of Politics*, Random House, Inc., New York, 1968), and "Fowler" (H. W. Fowler, *Dictionary of Modern English Usage*, Oxford University Press, New York, 1950). Authors of other books, as well as the titles of their works, are listed. So are newspaper and magazine writers, with separate entries for the periodicals where their material appeared. There is also occasional reference to items of general interest, such as "Prefixes" and "Suffixes," "Aesopian language," "Punctuation"; and to the originators, real or supposed, of individual words and expressions. Titles of relevant radio and television programs and of songs are listed as well.

Index of Words and Expressions